The Australian Women's Weekly cookbooks

Food editor *Pamela Clark*
Assistant food editor *Barbara Northwood*
Associate food editor *Enid Morrison*
Chief home economist *Jan Castorina*
Home economists *Jon Allen, Jane Ash,*
Karen Green, Sue Hipwell, Louise Patniotis,
Belinda Warn, Kathy Wharton
Editorial assistant *Denise Prentice*
Kitchen assistant *Amy Wong*

Designer *Lisa Rowell*
Stylists *Jacqui Hing, Carolyn Fienberg,*
Rosemary Ingram, Michelle Gorry
Photographers *Paul Clarke, Ashley Mackevicius,*
Andre Martin, Georgia Moxham

Home Library Staff
Editor-in-chief *Mary Coleman*
Designers *Michele Withers,*
Caryl Wiggins, Alison Windmill
Subeditor *Bianca Martin*
Editorial coordinators *Fiona Lambrou, Kate Neil*

Managing director *Colin Morrison*
Group publisher *Paul Dykzeul*

Produced by *The Australian Women's Weekly*
Home Library, Sydney.
Colour separations by ACP Colour Graphics Pty Ltd.
Printing by Times Printers Pte Limited, Singapore.
Published by ACP Publishing Pty Limited,
54 Park St, Sydney; GPO Box 4088, Sydney, NSW 1028.
Ph: (02) 9282 8618 Fax: (02) 9267 9438.
AWWHomeLib@publishing.acp.com.au

AUSTRALIA: Distributed by Network Distribution
Company, GPO Box 4088, Sydney, NSW 1028.
Ph: (02) 9282 8777 Fax: (02) 9264 3278.
UNITED KINGDOM: Distributed in the UK by
Australian Consolidated Press (UK),
20 Galowhill Rd, Brackmills, Northampton NN4 7EE,
(01604) 760 456.
CANADA: Distributed in Canada by Whitecap Books
Ltd, 351 Lynn Ave, North Vancouver, BC, V7J 2C4,
(604) 980 9852.
NEW ZEALAND: Distributed in New Zealand by
Netlink Distribution Company, 17B Hargreaves St,
Level 5, College Hill, Auckland 1, (9) 302 7616.
SOUTH AFRICA: Distributed in South Africa by
Intermag, PO Box 57394, Springfield 2137
Johannesburg, SA, (011) 491 7534.

Chocolate Cookbook
Includes index.
ISBN 0 949128 28 7
1. Cookery. Chocolate. (Series: Australian Women's
Weekly Home Library).
641.6'374

ACP Publishing Pty Limited 1998
ACN 053 273 546

Cover: Apricot Almond Layer Cake, page 26.
Opposite: Clockwise from top: Chocolate Nuts; Hazelnut
Clusters; Chocolate Ginger and Almond Dates, page 113.
Back cover: Clockwise from top left: Chocolate Nut Slice;
Chocolate Mallows; Coffee Thins;
Orange Thins, page 118.

Chocolate
COOKBOOK

For sheer indulgence, chocolate takes the cake—lots of cakes,
in fact, and very sumptuous they are, too. In this book,
we resisted no temptation at all when we carried chocolate to
new heights of glamour and style in cakes, desserts,
biscuits, slices and confectionery, all wickedly seductive.
For perfect results, first read our tips for success in
melting and handling chocolate on page 123—it's
simple when you know how.

Pamela Clark

FOOD EDITOR

BRITISH & NORTH AMERICAN READERS:
Please note that Australian cup and
spoon measurements are metric. A quick
conversion guide appears on page 128.
A glossary explaining unfamiliar terms
and ingredients appears on page 122.

Biscuits and Slices

Be tempted by our irresistible array of biscuits and slices — some crisp, some chewy, some luscious with cream, some packed with fruit and nuts (plus some always-popular unbaked slices). They are for every occasion that you want to make special.

CHOCOLATE TUILES

Tuiles are wafer-thin, elegant little biscuits to serve with coffee. At first they take practice to make perfect. Cook only 4 at a time on a tray because they must be curled quickly or they will set. Once you have established a cooking and curling time, you can cook 2 trays at a time, changing tray positions as you remove a tray from the oven and put in another tray. Tuiles can be made up to 2 days ahead; store in an airtight container. Recipe unsuitable to freeze or microwave.

1 egg white
¼ cup castor sugar
2 tablespoons plain flour
30g butter, melted
1 teaspoon vanilla essence
1 teaspoon cocoa
1 teaspoon milk
Beat egg white in small bowl until soft peaks form, add sugar gradually, beat until sugar is dissolved. Fold in sifted flour, cooled butter and essence in 2 batches. Place 2 tablespoonfuls of the mixture into another small bowl. Stir sifted cocoa and milk into the large batch of mixture.

Drop level teaspoonfuls of chocolate mixture about 10cm apart onto well-greased oven trays. Use back of teaspoon to spread mixture evenly to about 8cm diameter.

Clockwise from top left: Peppermint Macaroons, Chocolate Tuiles, Glacé Fruit Nuggets.

Bowls: Incorporated Agencies; background: washstand from Flossoms

Place plain mixture into piping bag fitted with small plain tube, pipe 3 lines across chocolate mixture. Using skewer, draw lines at 1cm intervals in alternate directions to give feathered effect (see glossary).

Bake in moderate oven for about 4 minutes or until tuiles set around edges. Lift tuiles carefully from tray with spatula, place immediately over rolling pin to curl. Leave few minutes until firm enough to remove from rolling pin.

Makes about 20.

GLACE FRUIT NUGGETS

Biscuits will keep for up to 2 weeks in an airtight container. Undecorated biscuits can be frozen for 2 months. Recipe unsuitable to microwave.

155g unsalted butter
⅓ cup castor sugar
1½ cups plain flour
½ teaspoon bicarbonate of soda
60g dark chocolate, melted
½ cup finely chopped mixed
    glacé fruit
60g dark chocolate, melted, extra
Combine butter and sugar in small bowl, beat with electric mixer until creamy. Stir in sifted flour and soda, then chocolate. Roll heaped teaspoonfuls of mixture into balls, make hollow in centre with thumb, push a little fruit into each hollow. Carefully roll biscuit dough around fruit, place about 3cm apart on lightly greased oven trays. Bake in moderately hot oven for about 10 minutes or until just firm; cool biscuits on trays. Pipe or drizzle extra chocolate over cold biscuits.

Makes about 40.

PEPPERMINT MACAROONS

Macaroons will keep well in an airtight container for up to a month. Recipe unsuitable to freeze or microwave.

3 egg whites
¾ cup castor sugar
1½ cups coconut
¼ teaspoon peppermint essence
60g White Melts, melted
125g dark chocolate, melted
Beat egg whites in small bowl with electric mixer until soft peaks form, gradually add sugar, beat until dissolved. Stir in coconut, essence and White Melts. Spoon mixture into piping bag with 1cm opening, pipe finger lengths about 2cm apart onto foil-covered trays. Bake in moderately slow oven for about 25 minutes or until firm; cool on trays. Drizzle or pipe dark chocolate over each macaroon.

Makes about 60.

TUILE ROLLS WITH WHITE CHOCOLATE FILLING

Biscuits can be made up to several hours before serving. First see recipe for Chocolate Tuiles on page 3 for hints on cooking tuiles. Recipe unsuitable to freeze or microwave.

TUILES
1 egg white
¼ cup castor sugar
¼ cup plain flour
30g butter, melted
½ teaspoon vanilla essence
WHITE CHOCOLATE FILLING
185g White Melts, melted
45g unsalted butter, melted
¼ cup thickened cream

ABOVE: Top: Tuile Rolls with White Chocolate Filling; bottom: Chocolate Nutty Surprises. RIGHT: Chocolate Almond Fancies.

Cloth: Jeffcoat Stevenson (above). Glass canister and plate: Incorporated Agencies; cloth: Jeffcoat Stevenson (right)

CHOCOLATE DIP
125g Milk Melts, melted
30g unsalted butter, melted
Tuiles: Beat egg white in small bowl until soft peaks form; add sugar gradually, beat until dissolved. Fold in sifted flour, cooled butter and essence in 2 batches. Drop level teaspoonfuls of mixture about 10cm apart onto well-greased oven trays; use back of teaspoon to spread each evenly to about 8cm diameter.

Bake in moderate oven for about 4 minutes or until tuiles brown around edges. Lift tuiles carefully from tray with a spatula, quickly shape around handle of a wooden spoon, leave to cool. Fit piping bag with a fluted tube, fill bag with white chocolate filling, pipe filling into each end of tuiles, allow to set at room temperature. Dip each end of biscuits into chocolate dip, place on foil-covered tray, allow biscuits to set at room temperature.

White Chocolate Filling: Mix all ingredients in small bowl until smooth.
Chocolate Dip: Combine Milk Melts and butter in bowl; stir until smooth.

Makes about 20.

CHOCOLATE NUTTY SURPRISES

Biscuits can be made up to 3 days ahead; store in airtight container. Undecorated biscuits can be frozen for up to 3 months. This recipe is unsuitable to microwave.

125g butter
½ teaspoon vanilla essence
½ cup castor sugar
1¾ cups plain flour
¼ cup packaged ground hazelnuts
30g Choc Bits, approximately
2 tablespoons castor sugar, extra
¼ teaspoon ground cinnamon
60g dark chocolate, melted
2 tablespoons flaked almonds, toasted, chopped
Combine butter, essence and sugar in small bowl, beat with electric mixer until light and fluffy; stir in sifted flour and hazelnuts. Roll level table-spoonfuls of mixture into sausage shapes, flatten slightly, press 3 Choc Bits into each piece of dough, reshape to enclose Choc Bits, toss in combined extra sugar and cinnamon.

Place about 2cm apart onto lightly greased oven trays, bake in moderate oven for about 12 minutes or until lightly browned. Remove from trays to wire rack to cool. Drizzle or pipe chocolate over biscuits, top biscuits with almonds.

Makes about 24.

CHOCOLATE ALMOND FANCIES

Biscuits can be made 2 days ahead; keep, covered, in refrigerator. Recipe unsuitable to freeze or microwave.

1¼ cups plain flour
¾ cup icing sugar
1 tablespoon cocoa
155g butter
½ cup packaged ground almonds
2 egg yolks
60g dark chocolate, melted
½ cup flaked almonds, toasted
2 tablespoons icing sugar, extra
Sift flour, icing sugar and cocoa into bowl, rub in butter. Add ground almonds and egg yolks, work with hand to make a firm dough. Knead gently on lightly floured surface until smooth, roll to 3mm thickness. Cut out rounds with 6cm cutter and place about 3cm apart on lightly greased oven trays.

Bake in moderate oven for about 12 minutes or until just firm. Lift onto wire racks to cool. Spread chocolate over each biscuit, press into flaked almonds, refrigerate until set. Sift extra icing sugar over half of each biscuit, decorate with more piped chocolate, if desired.

Makes about 30.

RUM CHOCOLATE CREAMS

Biscuits can be made up to 2 days ahead; store in airtight container. This recipe is unsuitable to freeze or microwave.

1⅓ cups plain flour
¼ cup cocoa
125g butter
⅓ cup castor sugar
1 egg, lightly beaten
2 tablespoons raspberry jam
2 teaspoons icing sugar
RUM BUTTER CREAM
1½ tablespoons water
¾ cup castor sugar
2 teaspoons dark rum
125g unsalted butter

Sift flour and cocoa into large bowl; rub in butter. Stir in sugar, then egg, mix with hand until combined, turn onto lightly floured surface, knead lightly until smooth. Roll mixture between sheets of plastic wrap in 2 or 3 batches. Cut out about 30 x 3cm rounds and about 30 x 5cm rounds; place about 2cm apart on lightly greased oven trays. Bake in moderate oven for about 12 minutes or until just firm. Lift onto wire rack to cool.

Spread large biscuits thinly with rum butter cream. Fit piping bag with small fluted tube, fill bag with remaining rum butter cream, pipe around edge of each large biscuit, place a little jam in centre of each.

Cover half top surface of each small biscuit with paper, dust other half with sifted icing sugar, place on top of each large biscuit, as shown.

Rum Butter Cream: Combine water and sugar in small saucepan, stir constantly over heat without boiling until sugar is dissolved, bring to boil, remove from heat; cool to room temperature, add rum. Beat butter in small bowl with electric mixer until as white as possible, add rum syrup in a thin stream to butter while mixer is operating; beat until combined.

Makes about 30.

CHOCOLATE WINDMILLS

Biscuits can be stored up to a week in an airtight container. Recipe unsuitable to freeze or microwave.

125g butter
½ cup castor sugar
1 egg, lightly beaten
2 tablespoons golden syrup
2 tablespoons cocoa
2½ cups self-raising flour
125g White Melts, melted
60g dark chocolate, melted

Cream butter and sugar in small bowl with electric mixer until light and fluffy. Add egg and syrup, beat until combined. Stir in sifted cocoa and flour. Turn onto floured surface, knead lightly until smooth. Cover dough, refrigerate for 30 minutes.

Roll dough thinly on lightly floured surface, cut out with 6cm square cutter. Make diagonal cut from each corner of dough to about 1cm from centre. Fold alternate points into centre, as shown.

Place biscuits about 5cm apart on lightly greased oven trays, bake in moderate oven for about 10 minutes or until just firm, lift onto wire rack to cool. Dip points of windmills into White Melts, return to wire rack to set. Drizzle with dark chocolate.

Makes about 36.

dough between sheets of greaseproof paper to about 3mm thick. Roll plain dough the same way.

Cut large shapes from plain dough and small shapes for centres from chocolate dough. Cut large shapes from chocolate dough and small shapes for centres from plain dough. Place large shapes about 2cm apart on lightly greased oven trays, place small centres to form contrast, as shown.

Bake in moderate oven for about 12 minutes or until lightly browned and just firm. Lift onto wire racks to cool. Spread a thin layer of the extra chocolate over flat side of biscuits.

Makes about 60.

CHOCOLATE PRETZELS

Pretzels will keep in an airtight container in refrigerator for up to a week. This recipe is unsuitable to freeze or microwave.

125g unsalted butter
1 teaspoon vanilla essence
½ cup castor sugar
1 egg
1 cup plain flour
¾ cup self-raising flour
2 tablespoons cocoa
1 egg white
100g dark chocolate, melted
15g unsalted butter, extra
1 tablespoon icing sugar

Combine butter, essence and sugar in small bowl, beat with electric mixer until light and fluffy, add egg, beat until combined, stir in sifted flours and cocoa. Turn dough onto lightly floured surface, knead lightly until smooth, cover, refrigerate 15 minutes.

Break pieces from dough, roll with fingers to sausage shapes about 5mm thick. Twist into pretzel shapes as shown, place about 2cm apart onto lightly greased oven trays, brush with

ABOVE: Clockwise from centre: Rum Chocolate Creams, Chocolate Windmills, Two-Tone Biscuits. RIGHT: Clockwise from top: Two-Tone Biscuits, Rocky Road Biscuits, Chocolate Pretzels, Chocolate Marshmallow Crowns.

Tiles: Northbridge Ceramic & Marble Centre (right)

TWO-TONE BISCUITS

Biscuits can be made up to 3 days ahead; store in airtight container. Use 2 cutter shapes of your choice for these pretty biscuits; make sure one cutter is larger than the other. Recipe unsuitable to freeze or microwave.

125g unsalted butter
1 teaspoon vanilla essence
⅔ cup castor sugar
1 egg
2¼ cups plain flour
50g dark chocolate, melted
200g dark chocolate, melted, extra

Cream butter, essence and sugar in small bowl with electric mixer until light and fluffy; add egg, beat until combined. Stir in sifted flour in 2 batches, knead gently on lightly floured surface until smooth.

Divide dough in half, wrap one half in plastic. Add chocolate to first half; work dough with fingers, kneading gently until combined. Roll chocolate

egg white. Bake in moderate oven for about 12 minutes or until just firm; lift onto wire racks to cool.

Combine chocolate and extra butter in small bowl, stir until smooth. Dip half of each pretzel into chocolate, place on waxed paper or foil until set. Dust other half of each pretzel with sifted icing sugar.

Makes about 40.

ROCKY ROAD BISCUITS

Biscuits will keep for up to a week in an airtight container in refrigerator. Uniced biscuits can be frozen for up to 2 months. This recipe is unsuitable to microwave.

125g unsalted butter
¾ cup icing sugar
1 cup plain flour
100g Rocky Road chocolate bar, chopped
¼ cup chocolate-coated peanuts, finely chopped
MARSHMALLOW ICING
100g packet white marshmallows
30g unsalted butter

Combine butter and sifted icing sugar in small bowl, beat with electric mixer until light and creamy. Stir in sifted flour, then chocolate. Roll rounded teaspoonfuls of mixture into balls, place about 5cm apart onto lightly greased oven trays; flatten slightly. Bake in moderately hot oven for about 10 minutes or until lightly browned; cool on tray. Spread tops with icing, sprinkle with peanuts.

Marshmallow Icing: Combine marshmallows and butter in saucepan, stir constantly over heat (or microwave on HIGH for about 1 minute) or until marshmallows are melted.

Makes about 30.

CHOCOLATE MARSHMALLOW CROWNS

Store biscuits in an airtight container in refrigerator for up to 2 days. Recipe unsuitable to freeze or microwave.

BISCUIT BASE
1 cup plain flour
1 tablespoon cocoa
90g butter
2 tablespoons castor sugar
1 egg, lightly beaten
2 teaspoons milk
CHERRY MARSHMALLOW
1 tablespoon gelatine
1 cup sugar
¾ cup water
1 teaspoon lemon juice
2 tablespoons chopped glacé cherries
CHOCOLATE COATING
200g dark chocolate, melted
60g unsalted butter, melted
Biscuit Base: Sift flour and cocoa into bowl, rub in butter, add sugar, egg and milk, mix to a firm dough. Roll level

tablespoonfuls of mixture into balls, place about 2cm apart onto lightly greased oven trays, flatten slightly with fork. Bake in moderate oven for about 15 minutes or until just firm; lift onto wire rack to cool.

Spoon marshmallow into piping bag fitted with a plain tube, pipe marshmallow onto biscuit bases; refrigerate until set. Dip marshmallow side of biscuits into chocolate coating, make sure marshmallow is covered.

Cherry Marshmallow: Mix gelatine and sugar together in saucepan, add water, stir constantly over heat, without boiling, until sugar is dissolved. Bring to boil, boil constantly, uncovered, for 6 minutes, without stirring. Remove from heat, cool to lukewarm. Pour mixture into large bowl, add lemon juice, beat with electric mixer until thick and creamy; stir in cherries.

Chocolate Coating: Stir chocolate and butter in small bowl until smooth.

Makes about 24.

CHOCOLATE COCONUT BISCUITS

Biscuits can be stored for up to 2 weeks in an airtight container. Recipe unsuitable to freeze or microwave.

125g butter, melted
1 teaspoon vanilla essence
½ cup castor sugar
1 egg
1½ cups self-raising flour
2 tablespoons cocoa
½ cup coconut
125g White Melts, melted
30g butter, melted, extra
1 cup coconut, extra

Combine butter, essence, sugar and egg in small bowl, beat with electric mixer until well combined. Stir in sifted flour and cocoa, then coconut. Roll rounded teaspoonfuls of dough into balls, place about 5cm apart on lightly greased oven trays. Bake in moderate oven for about 15 minutes or until just firm; cool on wire racks.

Combine White Melts and extra butter in bowl, dip top of each biscuit into mixture then into extra coconut. Drizzle or pipe tops with remaining chocolate mixture.

Makes about 30.

Chocolate Coconut Biscuits.

Glass horns: The Design Store; marble background: Appley Hoare Antiques

FRUITY WHITE CHOCOLATE BARS

Slice can be kept, covered, in refrigerator for a week or will freeze for up to 2 months. This recipe is unsuitable to microwave.

⅔ cup slivered almonds
1¼ cups (190g) brazil nuts, coarsely chopped
1½ cups coconut
1 cup chopped dried apricots
1 cup currants
¼ cup plain flour
250g white chocolate, melted
½ cup apricot jam
½ cup honey
1 tablespoon icing sugar

Lightly grease 19cm x 29cm lamington pan, cover base with greaseproof paper, grease paper. Combine nuts, coconut, fruit and flour in large bowl. Stir in combined hot chocolate, sieved jam and honey. Spread evenly into prepared pan; bake in moderately slow oven for 45 minutes. Cool in pan; dust with sifted icing sugar before cutting.

CHOCOLATE PISTACHIO BISCUITS

Biscuits can be stored for up to 2 weeks in an airtight container. Recipe unsuitable to freeze or microwave.

125g butter
2 tablespoons castor sugar
1¼ cups self-raising flour
⅓ cup full-cream milk powder
¼ cup sweetened condensed milk
125g dark chocolate, melted
125g dark chocolate, melted, extra
30g butter, melted, extra
½ cup pistachio nuts, chopped

Combine butter and sugar in small bowl, beat with electric mixer until light and fluffy. Stir in sifted flour and milk powder and condensed milk, then cooled chocolate. Roll rounded teaspoonfuls of mixture into balls, place about 5cm apart on lightly greased oven trays.

Bake in moderate oven for about 12 minutes or until just firm, lift onto wire rack to cool. Combine extra chocolate and extra butter in bowl.

Spread tops with chocolate mixture, sprinkle with nuts.

Makes about 30.

ABOVE: Fruity White Chocolate Bars.
RIGHT: Chocolate Pistachio Biscuits.

China: Sydney Antique Centre (above). Marble background: Appley Hoare Antiques (right)

CAPPUCCINO BROWNIES

Completed slice will keep up to 3 days in airtight container in the refrigerator. Uniced slice can be frozen up to 2 months. This recipe is unsuitable to microwave.

60g unsalted butter
1 teaspoon vanilla essence
½ cup brown sugar, firmly packed
2 eggs
½ cup plain flour
2 teaspoons dry instant coffee
250g dark chocolate, melted
⅔ cup macadamia nuts, chopped
1 tablespoon apricot jam
¼ teaspoon cocoa
¼ teaspoon icing sugar
VANILLA FROSTING
250g unsalted butter
1 teaspoon vanilla essence
1½ cups icing sugar

Grease 23cm square slab pan, cover base with foil, grease foil. Combine butter, essence and sugar in small bowl, beat with electric mixer until light and fluffy. Beat in eggs one at a time, beating well after each addition. Stir in sifted flour and coffee, cooled chocolate and nuts in 2 batches; spread into prepared pan. Bake in moderate oven for about 30 minutes or until firm; cool in pan.

Turn slice from pan, remove foil carefully, turn slice right way up. Brush hot sieved jam over slice, top with frosting; dust with combined sifted cocoa and icing sugar.

Vanilla Frosting: Cream butter and essence in small bowl with electric mixer until light and fluffy; beat in sifted icing sugar in several batches.

MACADAMIA PRALINE SLICE

Slice will keep up to 4 days in an airtight container in the refrigerator. This recipe is unsuitable to freeze or microwave.

BRANDY PRALINE
¼ cup sugar
2 tablespoons brandy
¾ cup macadamia nuts
CAKE LAYER
2 eggs
1 teaspoon vanilla essence
⅔ cup castor sugar
60g White Melts, melted
90g butter, melted
⅔ cup plain flour
100g dark chocolate, melted
15g butter, melted, extra
1 tablespoon icing sugar

Brandy Praline: Combine sugar and brandy in small heavy-based saucepan, stir constantly over heat, without boiling, until sugar is dissolved. Bring to boil, boil rapidly, uncovered, without stirring, for about 4 minutes or until sugar syrup turns light golden brown.

Add nuts, pour onto lightly greased oven tray (see glossary). When praline is cold, blend or process until finely chopped.

Cake Layer: Grease deep 20cm square cake pan, line with greaseproof or baking paper. Combine eggs, essence and sugar in small bowl, beat with electric mixer until thick and creamy. Gently stir in cooled White Melts and butter, then sifted flour and ⅔ of the praline. Pour into prepared pan. Bake in moderate oven for about 30 minutes or until firm; cool in pan.

Combine remaining praline, cooled dark chocolate and extra butter in small bowl, spread over slice. Dust with sifted icing sugar before serving.

CHOCOLATE TRIANGLES WITH MAPLE SYRUP GLAZE

Slice will keep for up to a week in an airtight container in the refrigerator. This recipe is unsuitable to freeze or microwave.

125g butter
2 teaspoons vanilla essence
¾ cup brown sugar, firmly packed
2 eggs
½ cup plain flour
¼ cup self-raising flour
¼ cup cocoa
¼ teaspoon bicarbonate of soda
½ cup chopped raisins
MAPLE SYRUP GLAZE
100g milk chocolate, chopped
¼ cup maple-flavoured syrup

Lightly grease 19cm x 29cm lamington pan. Combine butter, essence and sugar in small bowl, beat with electric mixer until light and fluffy. Add eggs, one at a time, beat until combined. Stir in sifted flours, cocoa and soda, then raisins.

Spread evenly into prepared pan, bake in moderate oven for about 25 minutes or until firm. Stand 5 minutes before spreading with glaze.

Maple Syrup Glaze: Combine chocolate and syrup in saucepan, stir constantly over heat, without boiling, until smooth. Use while warm.

From top: Cappuccino Brownies, Macadamia Praline Slice, Chocolate Triangles with Maple Syrup Glaze.

Glass plates: Dansab

PINEAPPLE CHOCOLATE SQUARES

Slice can be made up to 2 days ahead; keep, covered, in refrigerator. Recipe unsuitable to freeze or microwave.

125g butter
½ cup castor sugar
1 egg
1 cup plain flour
¼ cup self-raising flour
2 tablespoons cocoa
PINEAPPLE FILLING
450g can crushed pineapple
1½ tablespoons gelatine
¼ cup water
TOPPING
125g dark chocolate, melted
15g butter, melted

Grease 19cm x 29cm lamington pan, cover base with paper, grease paper. Combine butter and sugar in small bowl, beat with electric mixer until light and fluffy, add egg, beat until combined. Stir in sifted flours and cocoa in 2 batches, spread into prepared pan. Bake in moderate oven for about 20 minutes or until firm; cool in pan. When cold, spread with filling, then with topping.

Pineapple Filling: Blend or process undrained pineapple until finely chopped. Sprinkle gelatine over water, dissolve over hot water, stir into the pineapple.
Topping: Combine chocolate and butter in small bowl, stir until smooth.

GOLDEN COCONUT SLICE

Slice can be stored for up to 2 weeks in an airtight container. This recipe is unsuitable to freeze or microwave.

1 cup Corn Flakes
¼ cup coconut
185g butter
⅓ cup castor sugar
1¼ cups plain flour
1 tablespoon cocoa
200g White Melts, melted
90g butter, melted, extra
GOLDEN COCONUT TOPPING
½ cup golden syrup
60g butter
2 cups coconut

Combine Corn Flakes and coconut in frying pan, cook, stirring constantly, over heat for about 3 minutes or until Corn Flakes and coconut are golden brown; cool. Crush mixture until fine.

Combine butter and sugar in small bowl, beat with electric mixer until light and fluffy. Stir in sifted flour and cocoa, then Corn Flake mixture. Spread into lightly greased 19cm x 29cm lamington pan. Bake in moderate oven for 20 minutes.

Spread evenly with topping, bake further 10 minutes or until lightly browned, cool to room temperature. Spread evenly with combined White Melts and extra butter. Cut when set.
Golden Coconut Topping: Combine golden syrup and butter in saucepan, stir constantly over low heat, without boiling, until butter is melted. Stir in coconut, stir constantly over heat for about 3 minutes; use while warm.

ABOVE: Pineapple Chocolate Squares.
ABOVE RIGHT: Golden Coconut Slice.
RIGHT: Minty Mallow Slice.

Dish: Royal Copenhagen; table and cloth:
Sydney Antique Centre (above)
Plate: Orrefors (above right)

MINTY MALLOW SLICE

Slice will keep up to 3 days, covered, in refrigerator. Recipe unsuitable to freeze or microwave.

BASE
125g butter, melted
2 tablespoons cocoa
½ cup castor sugar
1 egg, lightly beaten
⅔ cup plain flour
300ml carton thickened cream
30g dark chocolate, grated
MINTY MALLOW FILLING
60g after-dinner mints
100g packet white marshmallows
90g unsalted butter
Base: Combine butter with sifted cocoa, sugar and egg in bowl; mix well. Stir in sifted flour. Spread evenly over base of greased 19cm x 29cm lamington pan. Bake in moderate oven for about 20 minutes or until firm, stand 5 minutes before spreading with filling; refrigerate until set. Beat 1 cup of the cream until soft peaks form, spread over filling, sprinkle with chocolate. Reserve remaining cream for filling.
Minty Mallow Filling: Combine mints, marshmallows, butter and remaining cream in saucepan, stir constantly over heat, without boiling, until smooth.

RUM RAISIN CARAMEL BARS

Bars can be made up to 4 days ahead. This recipe is unsuitable to freeze or microwave.

125g butter
½ cup castor sugar
1 cup plain flour
2 tablespoons cocoa
RUM AND RAISIN FILLING
400g can sweetened condensed milk
30g unsalted butter
1 tablespoon dark rum
½ cup chopped raisins
¼ cup coconut
TOPPING
125g dark chocolate, melted
30g butter, melted

Grease base and sides of 19cm x 29cm lamington pan, cover base with paper, grease paper. Combine butter and sugar in small bowl, beat with electric mixer until light and fluffy, stir in sifted flour and cocoa. Press evenly over base of prepared pan. Bake in moderate oven for about 15 minutes or until firm. Cool 10 minutes, spread with filling, cool to room temperature. Spread with topping, cut when set.

Rum and Raisin Filling: Combine condensed milk and butter in heavy-based saucepan, bring to boil while stirring constantly and vigorously over heat for about 10 minutes or until golden brown, remove from heat. Stir in rum, raisins and coconut, cool mixture to lukewarm.

Topping: Combine chocolate and butter in small bowl, stir until mixture is smooth and spreadable.

CHOCOLATE SHORTBREAD

We used Arnotts Scotch Finger Biscuits. Slice will keep for up to a week; keep, covered, in refrigerator. This recipe is unsuitable to freeze or microwave.

250g packet shortbread biscuits
200g unsalted butter
½ cup brown sugar
1 cup roasted hazelnuts, chopped
½ cup sultanas
¼ cup cocoa
1 egg, lightly beaten
1 tablespoon icing sugar

Line 19cm x 29cm lamington pan with foil. Cover base of prepared pan with biscuits in single layer.

Combine butter and sugar in saucepan, stir constantly over heat, without boiling, until sugar is dissolved; bring to boil, boil 1 minute, without stirring. Remove from heat, quickly stir in hazelnuts, sultanas, sifted cocoa and egg. Pour evenly over biscuits, refrigerate until set.

Remove slice from pan; place strips of paper across slice, dust with sifted icing sugar, carefully lift off paper before cutting.

CHOCOLATE PEANUTTIES

Slice can be made up to 3 days ahead or frozen for up to 2 months. Recipe unsuitable to microwave.

125g butter
¾ cup brown sugar, firmly packed
60g dark chocolate, chopped
2 tablespoons peanut butter
2 eggs
½ cup unsalted roasted peanuts, chopped
⅔ cup self-raising flour
1 tablespoon icing sugar

Grease deep 19cm square cake pan; cover base with paper, grease paper. Combine butter, brown sugar and chocolate in small saucepan, stir constantly over low heat until chocolate is melted; cool, do not allow to set. Combine peanut butter, eggs and peanuts in large bowl, stir in chocolate mixture and sifted flour. Pour into prepared pan, bake in moderate oven for about 30 minutes or until just firm. Stand 5 minutes before turning onto wire rack to cool. Dust with sifted icing sugar before cutting.

LEFT: From top: Chocolate Shortbread, Rum Raisin Caramel Bars. RIGHT: Chocolate Peanutties.

Dishes: Royal Copenhagen; tiles: The Slate People (left)
China: Royal Copenhagen; tiles: Old Balgowlah Restorations (right)

HEAVENLY RASPBERRY MARSHMALLOW SLICE

Slice can be prepared 2 days ahead; keep, covered, in refrigerator. Recipe unsuitable to freeze of microwave.

2 Weet-Bix biscuits, crushed
¾ cup self-raising flour
½ cup coconut
¼ cup brown sugar
60g dark chocolate, grated
100g butter, melted
1 egg, lightly beaten
RASPBERRY LAYER
400g raspberries
½ cup castor sugar
1 tablespoon gelatine
¼ cup water
MARSHMALLOW LAYER
1 tablespoon gelatine
1 cup castor sugar
¾ cup water
1 teaspoon vanilla essence
CHOCOLATE TOPPING
125g dark chocolate, melted
60g unsalted butter, melted

Grease 19cm x 29cm lamington pan, place strip of foil to cover base and extend over 2 opposite ends, grease foil thoroughly. Combine all ingredients in large bowl; mix well. Press over base of prepared pan. Bake in moderate oven for 15 minutes, allow base to cool in pan.

Pour raspberry layer over base, refrigerate until set. Spread marshmallow evenly over raspberry layer, refrigerate until set. Spread chocolate topping over marshmallow, refrigerate until set.

Raspberry Layer: Blend or process raspberries and sugar until smooth, sieve to remove seeds. Sprinkle gelatine over water, dissolve over hot water, stir into raspberry mixture.

Marshmallow Layer: Combine gelatine and sugar in medium saucepan, add water; stir constantly over low heat, without boiling, until sugar is dissolved. Bring to boil, boil gently, uncovered, without stirring, for 6

CHOCOLATE MINT SQUARES

Slice will keep in an airtight container in refrigerator for a week or will freeze for up to 2 months.

PEPPERMINT CREAM
60g butter
2 teaspoons peppermint essence
1 cup icing sugar
FILLING
½ cup slivered almonds, chopped
250g packet plain sweet biscuits, crushed
1 cup flaked coconut
1 cup icing sugar
¼ cup cocoa
100g dark chocolate, melted
250g butter, melted
TOPPING
200g dark chocolate, melted
30g butter, melted
1 tablespoon coconut

Peppermint Cream: Cover base of 19cm x 29cm lamington pan with foil. Beat butter and essence in small bowl with electric mixer until light and creamy, beat in sifted icing sugar gradually. Spread into prepared pan, freeze for 1 hour.

Filling: Combine almonds, biscuits, coconut, sifted icing sugar and cocoa in large bowl, stir in cooled chocolate and butter. Remove peppermint cream from freezer, chop into ½cm cubes. Quickly stir into chocolate mixture, press evenly back into the foil-lined lamington pan. Refrigerate for 1 hour.

Spread with topping, sprinkle with coconut, cover, refrigerate until set.
Topping: Combine chocolate and butter in small bowl: stir until smooth.

NUT CLUSTER BARS

Slice can be made up to 3 days ahead and kept in an airtight container in refrigerator or can be frozen for up to 2 months.

1 cup plain sweet biscuit crumbs
60g butter, melted
½ cup blanched almonds, chopped
⅓ cup pistachio nuts, chopped
¼ cup macadamia nuts, chopped
3 glacé pineapple rings, chopped
200g White Melts, melted
185g butter, melted, extra
200g dark chocolate, melted

In 19cm x 29cm lamington pan place strip of foil to cover base and extend over 2 opposite ends. Combine crumbs with butter in bowl, press evenly over base of prepared pan, refrigerate. Combine nuts and pineapple in bowl, mix well, divide nut mixture between 2 bowls.

Combine White Melts with ⅔ of the extra butter, stir into bowl of nut mixture; pour over biscuit base, refrigerate until set. Stir remaining butter and dark chocolate into remaining bowl of nut mixture, spread over white chocolate layer; cover, refrigerate until set.

minutes. Remove from heat, cool to lukewarm. Pour into small bowl, add essence, beat with electric mixer until thick and creamy.
Chocolate Topping: Combine chocolate and butter in small bowl; stir until smooth and spreadable.

ABOVE: Heavenly Raspberry Marshmallow Slice. RIGHT: From top: Chocolate Mint Squares, Nut Cluster Bars.

Glass plate: Dansab (above)
Tray: Lifestyle Imports (right)

COCONUT MARZIPAN SLICE

Slice can be prepared up to 4 days ahead; keep in an airtight container. This recipe is unsuitable to freeze or microwave.

125g unsalted butter
1 cup self-raising flour
2 tablespoons cocoa
½ cup castor sugar
¾ cup coconut
¼ cup packaged ground hazelnuts
¼ cup apricot jam
200g roll prepared marzipan
200g Milk Melts, melted
⅓ cup roasted hazelnuts, chopped

Grease 19cm x 29cm lamington pan, line base and sides with paper, grease paper. Melt butter in saucepan, stir in sifted flour and cocoa, sugar, coconut, and ground hazelnuts. Press into prepared pan, bake in moderate oven for about 15 minutes or until just firm; leave in pan.

Heat apricot jam in small saucepan, sieve. Roll marzipan between sheets of greaseproof paper; trim marzipan to same size as base of lamington pan.

Brush hot slice with jam, top with marzipan, cool in pan. Combine Milk Melts and chopped hazelnuts in bowl, spread over marzipan. Cut when cold.

ALMOND CHEESECAKE DELIGHTS

Slice will keep for up to a week, covered, in refrigerator. Recipe unsuitable to freeze or microwave.

200g dark chocolate, chopped
60g unsalted butter
½ cup castor sugar
2 eggs
¼ cup self-raising flour
¼ cup plain flour
¼ cup packaged ground almonds
¼ teaspoon almond essence
90g dark chocolate, melted, extra
30g unsalted butter, melted, extra
CHEESECAKE LAYER
125g packet cream cheese
30g unsalted butter
⅓ cup castor sugar
2 eggs
1 tablespoon plain flour
½ cup sour cream
1 teaspoon vanilla essence

Grease 19cm x 29cm lamington pan, cover base with paper, grease paper. Combine chocolate, butter and sugar in saucepan, stir constantly over low heat, without boiling, until chocolate is melted. Remove from heat, quickly stir in eggs, then sifted flours, almonds and essence. Spread mixture evenly into prepared pan, top evenly with cheesecake layer. Bake in moderate oven for about 45 minutes or until cheesecake is just set; cool in pan.

Spread cold slice evenly with combined extra chocolate and extra butter. Refrigerate until topping is set before cutting.

Cheesecake Layer: Combine cream cheese, butter and sugar in small bowl, beat with electric mixer until smooth. Beat in eggs one at a time, stir in flour, sour cream and essence.

CRUNCHY CRACKLE SLICE

Recipe can be made up to 3 days ahead; keep, covered, in refrigerator. Recipe unsuitable to freeze.

200g dark chocolate, melted
60g butter, melted
⅓ cup unsalted roasted peanuts, finely chopped
4 cups Rice Bubbles
125g butter, melted, extra
200g White Melts, melted

Into 19cm x 29cm lamington pan, place strip of foil long enough to cover base and extend over 2 opposite ends. Combine dark chocolate and butter in large bowl, stir until smooth. Stir in half the peanuts and half the Rice Bubbles. Spread evenly into prepared pan. Combine remaining peanuts, Rice Bubbles, extra butter and White Melts in large bowl; mix well. Spread evenly on top of dark chocolate layer, cover, refrigerate until set.

RIGHT, TOP: Almond Cheesecake Delights. RIGHT, BELOW: Crunchy Crackle Slice. BELOW: Coconut Marzipan Slice.

Dish: Royal Copenhagen (below)
Glass plate: Studio-Haus (right, top)

APRICOT GINGER FLORENTINES

Biscuits should be shaped quickly; first see recipe for Chocolate Tuiles on page 3 for hints on handling biscuits. Florentines can be made 2 weeks ahead; store in an airtight container. This biscuit recipe is unsuitable to freeze or microwave.

90g butter
1 cup slivered almonds,
   coarsely chopped
1/2 cup finely chopped
   dried apricots
1/4 cup finely chopped glace ginger
1 cup brown sugar, firmly packed
1/4 cup castor sugar
1/4 cup plain flour
150g dark chocolate, melted

Melt butter in saucepan, remove from heat, stir in almonds, apricots, ginger, sugars and flour. Drop rounded teaspoonfuls of mixture about 10cm apart onto oven trays which have been covered with baking powder. Bake in moderate oven for about 8 minutes or until lightly browned. Stand for about 2 minutes, remove from tray with spatula, place each biscuit over rolling pin to give curved shape. Drizzle or pipe chocolate over each biscuit, dust with sifted icing sugar, if desired.
   Makes about 20.

CHUNKY CHOCOLATE COOKIES

Biscuits can be stored in an airtight container for up to a week or frozen for up to 2 months. This recipe is unsuitable to microwave.

185g butter
1 teaspoon vanilla essence
1/4 cup castor sugar
1/3 cup brown sugar
1 egg
1 1/2 cups self-raising flour
200g dark chocolate, chopped

Combine butter, essence and sugars in small bowl, beat with electric mixer until light and fluffy; beat in egg. Stir in sifted flour and chocolate; cover, refrigerate 1 hour.
   Roll rounded teaspoonfuls of mixture quickly into balls, place about 5cm apart onto lightly greased oven trays. Bake in moderate oven for about 15 minutes or until lightly browned. Stand a few minutes before lifting onto wire racks to cool.
   Makes about 35.

HEAPS OF CHOCOLATE

Biscuits can be made up to 3 days ahead. Undecorated biscuits can be frozen for up to 3 months. Recipe unsuitable to microwave.

125g unsalted butter
1 cup brown sugar, firmly packed
50g dark chocolate, melted
2 eggs
1/4 cup cocoa
1 cup plain flour
3/4 cup self-raising flour
50g milk chocolate, chopped
50g white chocolate, chopped
60g slivered almonds
50g dark chocolate, melted, extra
50g white chocolate, melted, extra

Combine butter and sugar in small bowl, beat with electric mixer until light and fluffy, add cooled dark chocolate and eggs, beat until combined. Transfer mixture to large bowl, stir in sifted cocoa and flours in 2 batches, then milk and white chocolate and nuts. Drop heaped teaspoonfuls of mixture about 5cm apart onto lightly greased oven trays.
   Bake in moderate oven for about 10 minutes or until biscuits feel firm but slightly soft in the centre. Lift onto wire racks to cool. Drizzle or pipe with extra dark and white chocolate.
   Makes about 36.

CHERRY CHOCOLATE JUMBLES

Biscuits can be stored for up to a week in an airtight container or frozen for up to 2 months. This recipe is unsuitable to microwave.

60g butter
1 teaspoon vanilla essence
3/4 cup brown sugar, firmly packed
1 egg
1/2 cup sour cream
1 1/2 cups self-raising flour
1 cup walnuts or pecans, chopped
100g dark chocolate, chopped
1/2 cup red glacé cherries, chopped
1 tablespoon icing sugar

Combine butter, essence and sugar in small bowl, beat with electric mixer until light and fluffy; add egg, beat until well combined.
   Transfer mixture to large bowl. Stir in sour cream and sifted flour in 2 batches. Stir in nuts, chocolate and cherries. Cover, refrigerate mixture 30 minutes.
   Drop rounded teaspoonfuls of mixture about 5cm apart onto lightly greased oven trays. Bake in moderate oven for about 12 minutes or until lightly browned. Stand few minutes before lifting onto wire racks to cool. Dust lightly with sifted icing sugar just before serving.
   Makes about 60.

ABOVE: Apricot Ginger Florentines.
RIGHT: From top: Cherry Chocolate
Jumbles, Chunky Chocolate Cookies,
Heaps of Chocolate.

Tiles: Northbridge Ceramic & Marble
Centre (above)

Cakes

Few temptations are as delicious as the melting pleasures of a truly sumptuous chocolate cake, and here you will find a rich and varied extravaganza of such delights, including some cakes of surprising (but luscious) simplicity.

MOCHA TRUFFLE CAKE

Tia Maria and Kahlua are coffee-flavoured liqueurs. Cake can be made a day ahead. Recipe unsuitable to freeze or microwave.

3 eggs
½ cup castor sugar
¼ cup cornflour
¼ cup self-raising flour
¼ cup plain flour
2 tablespoons cocoa
2 tablespoons Tia Maria or Kahlua
2 tablespoons milk
2 x 300ml cartons thickened cream
100g white chocolate, melted
200g dark chocolate, melted
MILK CHOCOLATE TOPPING
200g milk chocolate, melted
90g unsalted butter, melted

Grease deep 23cm round cake pan, cover base with paper, grease paper. Beat eggs in small bowl with electric mixer until thick and creamy, gradually add sugar, beat until dissolved between each addition.

Transfer mixture to large bowl, lightly fold in sifted flours and cocoa, spread mixture into prepared pan. Bake in moderate oven for about 30 minutes or until firm, turn onto wire rack to cool. Split cake in half, brush with combined liqueur and milk.

Beat cream until soft peaks form; divide into 2 bowls. Quickly stir cooled white chocolate into one bowl of the cream and cooled dark chocolate into the remaining bowl of cream.

To assemble cake: Place strips of foil to cover base of deep cake pan and extend over edges or use 23cm springform tin. Place 1 cake half into pan or tin, spread cake with half the white chocolate cream, top with dark chocolate cream, then remaining white chocolate cream. Top with remaining cake. Refrigerate cake several hours or overnight, until firm. Carefully remove cake from pan or tin to serving plate. Spread cake with topping.

Milk Chocolate Topping: Combine hot chocolate and butter in bowl; stir until smooth. Cool to room temperature, stir occasionally until spreadable.

APRICOT SOUR CREAM CAKE

Cake is best prepared a day ahead; keep, covered, in refrigerator. Plain cake can be frozen for 2 months. Recipe unsuitable to microwave.

2 eggs
1 cup castor sugar
300g carton sour cream
100g dark chocolate, melted
1½ cups self-raising flour
APRICOT FILLING
¼ cup apricot jam
½ cup icing sugar
¼ cup packaged ground almonds
2 teaspoons lemon juice
SOUR CREAM GLAZE
100g dark chocolate, chopped
60g unsalted butter
½ cup icing sugar
¼ cup sour cream

Grease 15cm x 25cm loaf pan, cover base with paper, grease paper. Beat eggs and sugar in small bowl with electric mixer until thick and creamy, transfer to large bowl, stir in sour cream and cooled chocolate, lightly fold in sifted flour. Pour into prepared pan, bake in moderate oven for about 1½ hours or until firm. Stand 5 minutes before turning onto wire rack to cool.

Split cake into 3 layers, sandwich together with filling. Pour about half the cooled glaze over cake, allow remaining glaze to set to a spreadable consistency for piping. Decorate with flaked almonds.

Apricot Filling: Combine sieved jam, sifted icing sugar, almonds and lemon juice in bowl; stir until well combined.

Sour Cream Glaze: Combine chocolate, butter, icing sugar and cream in saucepan, stir constantly over heat until smooth. Bring to boil, boil 2 minutes, remove from heat, cool before using.

LEFT: Mocha Truffle Cake. RIGHT: Apricot Sour Cream Cake.

Plate: Ittala; fork: Novo Industries (left). China: Villeroy & Boch (right)

BLACK AND WHITE TORTE

Grand Marnier is an orange-flavoured liqueur. Torte can be made up to a day ahead. This recipe is unsuitable to freeze or microwave.

SPONGE
4 eggs
⅔ cup castor sugar
⅓ cup cornflour
⅓ cup plain flour
⅓ cup self-raising flour
⅓ cup Grand Marnier
DARK CHOCOLATE CREAM
300ml carton thickened cream
150g dark chocolate, chopped
1 tablespoon Grand Marnier
WHITE CHOCOLATE CREAM
2 x 300ml cartons thickened cream
300g white chocolate, chopped
2 tablespoons Grand Marnier
Sponge: Grease deep 23cm round cake pan. Beat eggs in medium bowl with electric mixer until thick and creamy, add sugar gradually, beating after each addition until sugar is dissolved; transfer to large bowl. Sift flours together 3 times, lightly fold into egg mixture.

Spread mixture evenly into prepared pan, bake in moderate oven for about 40 minutes or until firm. Turn sponge onto wire rack to cool.

Split cold cake into 3 layers; place 1 layer onto serving plate, brush with half the liqueur. Pipe alternating rings of dark and white chocolate cream to cover this layer. Add another layer, brush with remaining liqueur. Repeat piping on second layer with remaining dark chocolate cream and one-third of the remaining white chocolate cream. Top with the remaining cake layer. Spread cake all over with the remaining white chocolate cream. Decorate with fresh fruit and chocolate curls (see glossary).

Dark Chocolate Cream: Bring cream to boil in heavy-based saucepan, remove from heat, add chocolate and liqueur, stir until smooth. Transfer mixture to bowl, refrigerate 2 hours; beat with electric mixer until thick and creamy. Spoon mixture into piping bag fitted with plain tube.

With Chocolate Cream: Prepare as for dark chocolate cream.

APRICOT ALMOND LAYER CAKE

Cake can be made and iced up to 2 days ahead; keep, covered, in refrigerator. Amaretto is an almond-flavoured liqueur. Plain cake can be frozen for 2 months. This recipe is unsuitable to microwave.

155g unsalted butter
½ cup castor sugar
5 eggs, separated
150g dark chocolate, melted
1 tablespoon water
1 cup self-raising flour
⅓ cup packaged ground almonds
½ cup icing sugar
1 cup apricot jam
2 tablespoons Amaretto
CHOCOLATE ICING
125g unsalted butter, melted
125g dark chocolate, melted
Grease 2 deep 23cm round cake pans, cover bases with paper, grease paper. Combine butter and castor sugar in small bowl, beat with electric mixer until light and fluffy; beat in egg yolks 1 at a time, beat until combined. Transfer mixture to large bowl, stir in cooled chocolate and water, then sifted flour and almonds.

Beat egg whites in medium bowl until soft peaks form, add sifted icing sugar in several batches, beat until combined; fold lightly into chocolate mixture in 2 batches.

Divide mixture evenly between prepared pans. Bake in moderate oven for about 50 minutes or until firm. Stand 5 minutes before turning onto wire rack to cool to room temperature; leave cakes upside down.

Split cold cakes in half. Heat and sieve jam, combine with liqueur. Place 1 layer of cake onto serving plate. Sandwich cake layers together with jam mixture. Brush cake all over with remaining jam mixture. Stand about 1 hour at room temperature to allow jam mixture to set.

Spread cake all over with chocolate icing; allow cake to set at room temperature before cutting.

Chocolate Icing: Combine butter and chocolate in small bowl, stir until smooth; cool at room temperature, stirring occasionally, until icing is thick and spreadable.

ABOVE: Apricot Almond Layer Cake.
RIGHT: Black and White Torte.

China: Villeroy & Boch (above). China: The Bay Tree (right)

MOIST CHOCOLATE CARROT CAKE

Cake can be made up to 2 days ahead; keep, covered, in refrigerator. Plain cake can be frozen for 2 months. Recipe unsuitable to microwave.

185g butter
2 teaspoons grated orange rind
¾ cup castor sugar
2 eggs
1 tablespoon golden syrup
1½ cups coarsely grated carrot
1½ cups self-raising flour
½ teaspoon bicarbonate of soda
¼ cup cocoa
¾ cup milk
CREAM CHEESE FROSTING
125g packet cream cheese
60g butter
1 teaspoon coarsely grated
    orange rind
3 cups icing sugar
2 teaspoons hot water

Grease 20cm baba pan. Cream butter, rind and sugar in small bowl with electric mixer only until combined. Beat in eggs and golden syrup, transfer to large bowl. Stir in carrot, sifted flour, soda, cocoa and milk in 2 batches.

Pour mixture into prepared pan. Bake in moderate oven for about 50 minutes or until firm. Stand 5 minutes before turning onto wire rack to cool. Spread cold cake with frosting.

Cream Cheese Frosting: Beat cream cheese, butter and orange rind in small bowl with electric mixer until light and fluffy, gradually beat in sifted icing sugar and water; beat until combined.

PEPPERMINT CHOCOLATE RING

Creme de Menthe is a mint-flavoured liqueur. Cake can be made up to a day ahead; keep, covered, in refrigerator. Uniced cake can be frozen for up to 2 months. This recipe is unsuitable to microwave.

⅓ cup water
80g dark chocolate
90g butter
½ cup castor sugar
2 eggs
⅓ cup sour cream
1 cup self-raising flour
1 tablespoon Creme de Menthe
1 teaspoon water, extra
PEPPERMINT CREAM
90g unsalted butter
1½ cups icing sugar
3 teaspoons milk
peppermint essence
green colouring
CHOCOLATE TOPPING
150g dark chocolate, melted
125g unsalted butter, melted

Grease and flour 24cm savarin tin or 20cm ring pan. Combine water and chocolate in small saucepan, stir over low heat until smooth, cool.

Cream butter and sugar in small bowl with electric mixer until light and fluffy, add eggs 1 at a time, beating well after each addition. Transfer mixture to large bowl, stir in chocolate mixture, sour cream and sifted flour in 2 batches. Spread mixture into prepared pan; bake in moderate oven for about 30 minutes or until firm. Stand cake 5 minutes before turning onto wire rack to cool.

Brush cold cake with combined liqueur and extra water. Fit a piping bag with fluted tube, fill bag with peppermint cream, pipe cream over top of cake; refrigerate until firm. Place cake onto wire rack with tray underneath, pour topping evenly over cake, refrigerate until set.

Peppermint Cream: Beat butter in small bowl with electric mixer until as white as possible; gradually beat in sifted icing sugar, then milk. Flavour icing with essence and colour green to desired strength.

Chocolate Topping: Stir chocolate and butter together in bowl until smooth and pourable.

LEFT: Moist Chocolate Carrot Cake.
ABOVE: Peppermint Chocolate Ring.

China: Michael A. Green Antiques; cloth: Balmain Linen & Lace (left). China: Limoges (above)

CHOCOLATE CHIP FRUIT CAKE

Cake will keep for up to a month in an airtight container or will freeze for up to 3 months. This recipe is unsuitable to microwave.

2¼ cups (375g) sultanas
1 cup glacé cherries, halved
1 cup chopped glacé apricots
150g dark chocolate, chopped
185g butter, chopped
¾ cup brown sugar, firmly packed
1 cup sweet sherry
4 eggs, lightly beaten
155g Choc Bits
1¾ cups plain flour
¼ cup self-raising flour
½ teaspoon bicarbonate of soda
2 tablespoons sweet sherry, extra

Combine fruit, chocolate, butter, sugar and sherry in large saucepan, stir constantly over heat, without boiling, until chocolate and butter are melted. Bring to boil, reduce heat, simmer, uncovered, for 10 minutes. Transfer mixture to large bowl; allow to cool to room temperature.

Grease deep 19cm square cake pan, line base and sides with 2 thicknesses greaseproof paper, bringing paper 2cm above edge of pan.

Stir eggs into fruit mixture, then Choc Bits, sifted flours and soda.

Spread evenly into prepared pan, bake in slow oven for about 2 hours. Brush with extra sherry, cover tightly with foil; cool in pan.

TORTE ROYALE

Ground almonds replace the flour in this rich torte. Tia Maria and Kahlua are coffee-flavoured liqueurs. Torte can be made up to 3 days ahead; keep, covered, in refrigerator. Cake can be frozen for 2 months. Recipe unsuitable to microwave.

100g dark chocolate, melted
100g unsalted butter, melted
1 tablespoon Tia Maria or Kahlua
1 tablespoon dry instant coffee
2 tablespoons hot water
⅔ cup castor sugar
⅔ cup packaged ground almonds
3 eggs, separated
1 tablespoon icing sugar

Grease deep 20cm round cake pan, cover base with paper, grease paper. Combine chocolate, butter, liqueur, combined coffee and water, sugar and almonds in large bowl; stir until combined. Stir in egg yolks 1 at a time.

Beat egg whites in small bowl until soft peaks form, fold lightly into chocolate mixture, spread into prepared pan. Bake in moderate oven

for 45 minutes or until firm. Cool in pan, carefully turn cake from pan, dust with sifted icing sugar. Serve with whipped cream, if desired.

WHITE CHOCOLATE RIPPLE CAKE

Cake will keep for 2 days, covered, in refrigerator. Recipe unsuitable to freeze or microwave.

125g butter
1 cup castor sugar
2 eggs
1⅓ cups self-raising flour
2 tablespoons cocoa
½ cup water
WHITE CHOCOLATE RIPPLE
100g white chocolate, melted
125g ricotta cheese
1 egg
2 teaspoons plain flour
1 teaspoon vanilla essence
SOUR CREAM FROSTING
125g dark chocolate, melted
¼ cup sour cream
½ cup icing sugar

Grease 20cm ring pan, cover base with paper, grease paper. Combine butter, sugar, eggs, sifted flour and cocoa and water in medium bowl, beat on low speed with electric mixer until ingredients are combined. Increase

speed to medium, beat for 3 minutes or until mixture is changed in colour and smooth.

Pour ⅔ mixture into prepared pan, spread evenly with white chocolate ripple mixture, then spread with remaining cake mixture. Bake in moderate oven for about 45 minutes or until firm. Cool to room temperature in pan before turning onto wire rack. Spread cake all over with frosting.

White Chocolate Ripple: Combine all ingredients in small bowl, beat with electric mixer until smooth.

Sour Cream Frosting: Combine hot chocolate and sour cream in small bowl, stir until smooth. Stir in sifted icing sugar. Refrigerate frosting until thick and spreadable.

ABOVE: Chocolate Chip Fruit Cake.
ABOVE, RIGHT: Torte Royale. RIGHT:
White Chocolate Ripple Cake.

China: Sydney Antique Centre (above, left).
China: Villeroy & Boch; glass: Mikasa (above, right). Plate: Royal Copenhagen; tiles: The Slate People (right, below)

PEACHY LIQUEUR DREAM CAKE

Cake is best prepared several hours ahead; keep, covered, in refrigerator. Plain cake can be frozen for 2 months. Recipe unsuitable to microwave.

185g unsalted butter
2 teaspoons grated orange rind
¾ cup castor sugar
3 eggs
100g white chocolate, melted
2 cups self-raising flour
¾ cup water
300ml carton thickened cream
¼ cup icing sugar
½ cup packaged ground hazelnuts

PEACHY LIQUEUR FILLING
2 medium peaches, chopped
2 tablespoons peach liqueur
300ml carton thickened cream
¼ cup icing sugar

Grease deep 23cm round cake pan, cover base with paper, grease paper. Cream butter, rind and sugar in small bowl with electric mixer until light and fluffy. Add eggs 1 at a time, beating well after each addition; beat in cooled chocolate. Transfer mixture to large bowl, stir in sifted flour and water in 2 batches.

Spread into prepared pan, bake in moderately slow oven for about 1½ hours or until firm. Stand cake 5 minutes before turning onto wire rack to cool.

Split cake into 3 layers, sandwich layers together with filling; place onto serving plate. Whip cream and sifted icing sugar in small bowl until soft peaks form. Spread and decorate cake with cream. Press hazelnuts onto side of cake. Decorate cake with toffee, if desired (see glossary).

Peachy Liqueur Filling: Combine peaches with liqueur in bowl, stand for 30 minutes. Whip cream and sifted icing sugar in small bowl until soft peaks form, fold in peach mixture.

32

CHOCOLATE BUTTERMILK CAKE

Cake can be made up to a day ahead; keep, covered, in refrigerator. Plain cake can be frozen for up to 2 months. Recipe unsuitable to microwave.

185g butter
1 teaspoon vanilla essence
1½ cups castor sugar
4 eggs, separated
¾ cup self-raising flour
⅓ cup cocoa
¾ cup buttermilk
300ml carton thickened cream
CHOCOLATE FILLING
200g dark chocolate, melted
90g butter, melted

Grease deep 23cm round cake pan, cover base with paper, grease paper. Cream butter, essence and sugar in small bowl with electric mixer until light and fluffy; beat in egg yolks until just combined. Transfer mixture to large bowl; stir in sifted flour and cocoa and buttermilk. Beat egg whites in small bowl with electric mixer until soft peaks form, lightly fold through cake mixture in 2 batches.

Pour mixture into prepared pan, bake in moderate oven for about 1 hour or until firm. Turn onto wire rack to cool.

Split cake in half, sandwich together with about half the filling, place onto serving plate, spread and decorate top with remaining filling. Beat cream until firm peaks form, spread side of cake with dream.

Chocolate Filling: Combine chocolate and butter in small bowl, stir until smooth; stand until spreadable.

LEFT: Peachy Liqueur Dream Cake.
BELOW: Chocolate Buttermilk Cake.

Cake stand: Mikasa (left). China: Studio-Haus; cloth: Balmain Linen and Lace (below)

HONEY CREAM CHOCOLATE SPONGE

It is correct that this sponge contains plain flour. Tia Maria and Kahlua are coffee-flavoured liqueurs. Recipe can be made up to 2 days ahead; keep, covered, in refrigerator. Unfilled sponge can be frozen for up to a month. This recipe is unsuitable to microwave.

4 eggs
⅔ cup castor sugar
1 cup plain flour
2 tablespoons cocoa
COFFEE LIQUEUR SYRUP
¼ cup sugar
¼ cup water
2 tablespoons Tia Maria or Kahlua
HONEY CREAM
250g unsalted butter
½ cup honey

Grease base of 20cm springform tin, cover base with paper, grease paper. Combine eggs in medium bowl, beat with electric mixer until thick and fluffy; add sugar gradually, beat until dissolved between each addition. Sift flour and cocoa together 3 times, fold into egg mixture in 2 batches.

Spread ½ cup mixture evenly over base of tin, bake in moderate oven for about 7 minutes or until just firm; turn onto wire rack to cool. Repeat with remaining mixture. Brush each cake layer with syrup. Sandwich layers together with a little of the honey cream. Spread cake all over with remaining honey cream. Decorate with chocolate leaves (see glossary).

Coffee Liqueur Syrup: Combine sugar and water in small saucepan, stir constantly over heat, without boiling, until sugar is dissolved; bring to boil, remove from heat, cool to room temperature. Stir in liqueur.

Honey Cream: Beat butter in small bowl with electric mixer until as white as possible; beat in honey.

CHOCOLATE PEANUT BUTTER CAKE

Cake can be made a day ahead; keep, covered, in refrigerator. Plain cake can be frozen for 2 months. Recipe unsuitable to microwave.

90g butter
1 teaspoon vanilla essence
2 tablespoons smooth peanut butter
⅔ cup brown sugar, firmly packed
3 eggs, separated
¾ cup self-raising flour
⅔ cup plain flour
¾ cup milk
CARAMEL CREAM FILLING
300ml carton thickened cream
2 tablespoons caramel topping
CHOCOLATE FROSTING
¼ cup castor sugar
¼ cup water
2 egg yolks
100g dark chocolate, melted
60g butter, softened

Grease deep 23cm round cake pan, cover base with paper, grease paper.

ABOVE: Honey Cream Chocolate Sponge. RIGHT: Chocolate Almond Liqueur Cake. RIGHT, BELOW: Chocolate Peanut Butter Cake.

China: Dansab; table: Australian East India Co. (above). Tiles: Pazotti (right)

Cream butter, essence, peanut butter and sugar in small bowl with electric mixer until light and fluffy. Add egg yolks, beat until combined; transfer to large bowl. Stir in sifted flours and milk in 2 batches. Beat egg whites until soft peaks form, fold lightly through cake mixture in 2 batches.

Pour mixture into prepared pan, bake in moderate oven for about 45 minutes or until firm. Stand few minutes before turning onto wire rack to cool. Split cake into 3 layers, sandwich layers together with filling. Refrigerate for at least 1 hour before spreading with frosting.

Caramel Cream Filling: Beat cream and topping in small bowl with electric mixer until firm peaks form.

Chocolate Frosting: Combine sugar and water in saucepan, stir constantly over heat, without boiling, until sugar is dissolved; bring to boil, boil, uncovered, without stirring, for 1 minute. Beat egg yolks in small bowl with electric mixer until thick and creamy, gradually beat in the hot sugar syrup while motor is operating. Add chocolate and butter, beat until frosting is thick and smooth.

CHOCOLATE ALMOND LIQUEUR CAKE

Grand Marnier is an orange-flavoured liqueur. Almonds replace flour in this cake. Cake can be made up to 3 days ahead; keep, covered, in refrigerator. Plain cake can be frozen for 2 months. Recipe unsuitable to microwave.

400g dark chocolate, melted
250g unsalted butter, melted
¼ cup water
⅓ cup Grand Marnier
6 eggs, separated
1 cup castor sugar
2 cups (240g) packaged ground almonds
CHOCOLATE GLAZE
250g dark chocolate, melted
1 cup thickened cream

Grease deep 23cm square cake pan, cover base with paper, grease paper. Combine chocolate, butter, water and liqueur in large bowl, stir until smooth. Beat egg yolks and sugar in small bowl with electric mixer until thick and pale; fold into chocolate mixture with almonds. Beat egg whites in medium bowl with electric mixer until soft peaks form, fold egg whites into chocolate mixture in 2 batches.

Pour into prepared pan, bake in moderate oven for about 1¼ hours or until firm; cool cake in pan. Turn cake onto serving plate, cover cake with glaze; refrigerate until required. Decorate with chocolate curls, if desired (see glossary).

Chocolate Glaze: Combine chocolate and cream in bowl; stir until smooth. Refrigerate until glaze is thick and pourable.

DEVILISHLY DARK CHOCOLATE TORTE

Crème de Cacao is a chocolate-flavoured liqueur. Cake can be made 2 days ahead; keep, covered, in refrigerator. Plain cake can be frozen for 2 months. This recipe is unsuitable to microwave.

185g butter
3 teaspoons dry instant coffee
1 cup hot water
150g dark chocolate, chopped
1½ cups castor sugar
1 cup self-raising flour
¾ cup plain flour
2 tablespoons cocoa
2 eggs
1 teaspoon vanilla essence
2 teaspoons raspberry jam
2½ tablespoons Crème de Cacao
¾ cup flaked almonds, toasted, chopped
15g dark chocolate, melted, extra
DARK CHOCOLATE FILLING
200g dark chocolate, melted
125g unsalted butter, melted
¼ cup icing sugar

Grease base and sides of deep 23cm square cake pan, cover base with paper, grease paper.

Melt butter in saucepan, remove from heat, stir in combined coffee and hot water, then chocolate and sugar; stir until smooth. Place into large bowl of electric mixer, beat in sifted dry ingredients in 3 batches. Beat in eggs and essence.

Pour into prepared pan, bake in slow oven for about 1¼ hours or until firm. Stand 5 minutes before turning onto wire rack to cool.

Split cake in half, split each half into 3 layers. Reserve ⅔ cup filling.

Place a layer of cake onto serving plate, spread thinly with jam then a thin layer of filling. Top with another layer of cake, sprinkle with a little of the liqueur, then spread thinly with filling. Repeat layering with remaining cake, liqueur and filling. Refrigerate several hours or until firm.

Spread reserved filling all over cake, press almonds onto sides. While top of cake is soft, pipe lines of extra chocolate about 2cm apart crossways on cake. Pull skewer through chocolate lines at 2cm intervals in alternate directions to give feathered effect (see glossary).

Dark Chocolate Filling: Combine hot chocolate and butter in bowl, stir in sifted icing sugar, cool to room temperature; beat with wooden spoon until thick and spreadable.

MOIST COFFEE CAKE WITH CHOCOLATE SYRUP

Cake can be kept, covered, in refrigerator for up to 3 days. Recipe unsuitable to freeze or microwave.

⅓ cup water
1 tablespoon dry instant coffee
¾ cup sugar
125g butter
3 eggs, separated
1½ cups self-raising flour

CHOCOLATE SYRUP
1 cup sugar
⅔ cup water
50g dark chocolate, chopped

Grease 20cm baba or ring pan. Combine water and coffee in small saucepan, add sugar; stir constantly over heat, without boiling, until sugar is dissolved. Bring to boil, remove from heat, cool syrup to room temperature.

Combine butter and egg yolks in small bowl, beat with electric mixer until light and creamy. Gradually pour sugar syrup in a thin stream into butter mixture while motor is operating. Transfer mixture to large bowl; stir in sifted flour. Beat egg whites in small bowl until soft peaks form; fold into butter mixture in 2 batches.

Spread into prepared pan, bake in moderate oven for about 40 minutes or until firm. Stand few minutes before turning onto wire rack over tray. Brush hot cake with hot syrup.

Chocolate Syrup: Combine sugar and water in small saucepan, stir constantly over heat, without boiling, until sugar is dissolved; bring to boil, reduce heat, simmer, uncovered, without stirring, for 3 minutes. Add chocolate, stir until completely melted.

ABOVE: Devilishly Dark Chocolate Torte.
RIGHT: Moist Coffee Cake with Chocolate Syrup.

China: Villeroy & Boch; table: Wentworth Antiques (above)

CHOCOLATE POPPY SEED CAKE

Cake is best assembled several hours before required; keep, covered, in refrigerator. Plain cake will freeze for 2 months. This recipe is not suitable to microwave.

125g butter
½ cup castor sugar
8 eggs, separated
¾ cup stale breadcrumbs
1 cup poppy seeds
300g dark chocolate, melted
¼ cup plum jam
RICH CREAM GLAZE
⅔ cup thickened cream
200g dark chocolate, melted

Grease base and side of deep 23cm round cake pan, cover base with paper, grease paper. Combine butter and sugar in small bowl, beat with electric mixer until light and fluffy; add egg yolks 1 at a time, beat until combined. Transfer to large bowl, stir in breadcrumbs, poppy seeds and cooled chocolate.

Beat egg whites in large bowl with electric mixer until soft peaks form, fold into chocolate mixture in 2 batches; pour into prepared pan. Bake in moderately slow oven for about 1¼ hours or until firm; cool in pan.

Trim top of cake to make flat, split cake into 2 layers. Place 1 layer onto serving plate, spread with sieved jam, top with remaining layer of cake. Spread glaze all over cake, refrigerate until set.

Rich Cream Glaze: Combine cream and chocolate in small bowl; stir until smooth and pourable.

CHOCOLATE BERRY BLISS

This flourless cake will keep well, covered, in refrigerator for a week; it will freeze for 2 months. Recipe unsuitable to microwave.

8 eggs, separated
1 cup castor sugar
¼ cup cocoa
2 teaspoons vanilla essence
200g dark chocolate, melted
TOPPING
150g white chocolate, melted
30g butter, melted
STRAWBERRY SAUCE
250g punnet strawberries
1 tablespoon strawberry jam
2 tablespoons icing sugar

Lightly grease base and side of 20cm springform tin. Cover base with paper, grease paper. Combine egg yolks and sugar in small bowl, beat with electric mixer until thick and creamy. Beat in sifted cocoa, essence and cooled chocolate; transfer to large bowl. Beat egg whites in large bowl until soft peaks form, fold into chocolate mixture in 2 batches.

Pour into prepared tin, bake in moderate oven for about 45 minutes or until firm. Stand 10 minutes before turning onto wire rack to cool. Drizzle or pipe topping over cake; serve with strawberry sauce.

Topping: Combine chocolate and butter in small bowl, stir until topping is smooth.

Strawberry Sauce: Blend or process strawberries, jam and icing sugar until smooth; sieve before using.

ABOVE: Chocolate Berry Bliss. BELOW: Chocolate Poppy Seed Gateau. RIGHT: Almond Meringue Cake.

Plate: Ittala (above). Plate: Studio-Haus (below). China: Limoges (right)

ALMOND MERINGUE CAKE

Amaretto is an almond-flavoured liqueur. Cakes can be cooked together; place pans about 3cm apart. Completed cake can be made a day ahead; keep, covered, in refrigerator. This recipe is unsuitable to freeze or microwave.

125g butter
½ teaspoon almond essence
½ cup castor sugar
3 egg yolks
1 cup self-raising flour
⅓ cup cocoa
½ cup buttermilk
½ cup sour cream
2 tablespoons flaked almonds

MERINGUE
3 egg whites
⅔ cup castor sugar
ALMOND CREAM
300ml carton thickened cream
1 tablespoon Amaretto
2 tablespoons icing sugar
30g white chocolate, grated

Grease 2 deep 20cm round cake pans, cover bases with paper, grease paper. Combine butter, essence, sugar, egg yolks in small bowl, beat with electric mixer until light and fluffy. Transfer to large bowl, stir in sifted flour with cocoa and combined buttermilk and sour cream in 2 batches.

Divide mixture evenly between prepared pans. Spread top of 1 mixture with meringue, sprinkle with almonds, bake in moderate oven for 25 minutes, cover top of cake loosely with foil, bake further 15 minutes, stand 5 minutes before turning onto wire rack. Turn cake right way up to cool.

Bake plain mixture in moderate oven for about 25 minutes or until firm, turn onto wire rack to cool. Sandwich cakes together with almond cream.

Meringue: Beat egg whites in small bowl with electric mixer until soft peaks form, gradually add sugar, beat until dissolved between each addition.

Almond Cream: Beat cream, liqueur and sifted icing sugar together in small bowl with electric mixer until firm peaks form; stir in chocolate.

CHOCOLATE SUPREME CAKE

Crème de Cacao is a chocolate-flavoured liqueur. Cake can be prepared 2 days ahead; store, covered, in refrigerator. Plain cake can be frozen for 2 months. Recipe unsuitable to microwave.

125g butter
1¼ cups castor sugar
2 eggs
⅔ cup plain flour
⅔ cup self-raising flour
⅓ cup cocoa
½ cup sour cream
½ cup water
CHOCOLATE CREAM
⅓ cup castor sugar
¼ cup Crème de Cacao
¼ cup water
200g unsalted butter
200g dark chocolate, melted
CREAMY TOPPING
200g dark chocolate, melted
⅔ cup thickened cream

Grease base and side of deep 23cm round cake pan, cover base with paper, grease paper. Combine butter and sugar in small bowl, beat with electric mixer until light and fluffy, beat in eggs 1 at a time. Transfer mixture to large bowl, stir in combined sifted flours and cocoa, and combined sour cream and water in 2 batches.

Spread into prepared pan, bake in moderate oven for about 50 minutes or until firm. Stand 10 minutes before turning onto wire rack to cool; leave cake upside down for decorating.

Reserve ¾ cup chocolate cream for decorating. Spread remaining cream evenly all over cake; refrigerate for 1 hour or until cream is firm. Place cake on wire rack over a tray. Quickly and carefully spread topping all over cake; refrigerate for 1 hour or until set. Lift cake onto serving plate, decorate with reserved cream.

Chocolate Cream: Combine sugar, liqueur and water in small saucepan, stir constantly over heat, without boiling, until sugar is dissolved; bring to boil, remove from heat, allow to cool to room temperature.

Beat butter in small bowl with electric mixer until light and fluffy; gradually beat in cold sugar syrup while mixer is operating, then gradually beat in cooled chocolate.

Creamy Topping: Combine chocolate and cream in bowl; stir until smooth.

RIGHT: Chocolate Supreme Cake. FAR RIGHT: Chocolate Walnut Log.

China: Limoges; background table: Suko (right). Glassware: Dansab; table: Kerry Trollope Antiques (far right)

CHOCOLATE WALNUT LOG

Log can be prepared up to 1 day ahead; keep, covered, in refrigerator. Plain log can be frozen for 2 months. Recipe unsuitable to microwave.

125g butter
¾ cup castor sugar
2 eggs
½ cup plain flour
¾ cup self-raising flour
¼ cup cocoa
⅓ cup milk
½ cup walnuts, chopped
CHOCOLATE BRANDY CREAM
125g unsalted butter
¼ cup icing sugar
200g White Melts, melted
2 tablespoons brandy

Grease 2 nut roll tins. Combine butter and sugar in small bowl, beat with electric mixer until light and fluffy; beat in eggs 1 at a time. Transfer to large bowl. Stir in sifted flours and cocoa with milk and walnuts in 2 batches.

Divide mixture between prepared tins. Bake in moderate oven for 50 minutes. Stand rolls in tins with lids for 10 minutes, remove lids, turn onto wire rack to cool. Trim ends from rolls, trim side of each roll so the rolls will sit flat.

Cut roll into 1cm slices, join with thin layer of chocolate cream. Place roll on serving plate, refrigerate 2 hours. Spread roll with remaining cream, serve sliced diagonally. Decorate

with chocolate leaves, if desired (see glossary).

Chocolate Brandy Cream: Cream butter and sifted icing sugar in small bowl with electric mixer until light and fluffy; beat in cooled chocolate and brandy. Refrigerate, stirring occasionally until spreadable.

DATE AND CHOCOLATE TORTE

Torte is best served on the day it is made. This recipe is unsuitable to freeze or microwave.

3 egg whites
½ cup castor sugar
1 cup slivered almonds, finely chopped
¾ cup finely chopped dates
125g dark chocolate, grated
300ml carton thickened cream
50g dark chocolate, grated, extra

Grease 23cm springform tin, cover base with foil, grease foil. Beat egg whites in small bowl with electric mixer until soft peaks form, gradually add sugar, beat until dissolved between each addition. Fold in almonds, dates and chocolate.

Spread mixture into prepared tin, bake in moderately slow oven for about 40 minutes or until firm; cool in tin. Turn out, remove foil, turn right way up on serving plate. Cover top with whipped cream, decorate with extra grated chocolate. Refrigerate several hours before serving.

CHOCOLATE MOUSSE SPONGE

Cake can be made up to a day ahead; store, covered, in refrigerator. Recipe unsuitable to freeze or microwave.

3 eggs
⅓ cup castor sugar
1 teaspoon vanilla essence
⅓ cup self-raising flour
¼ cup packaged ground almonds
50g dark chocolate, grated
1 tablespoon icing sugar
250g punnet strawberries
CHOCOLATE MOUSSE
¼ cup thickened cream
100g dark chocolate, grated
1 teaspoon vanilla essence
3 teaspoons gelatine
¼ cup water
4 egg whites
¼ cup castor sugar

Grease deep 23cm round cake pan, cover base with paper, grease paper. Combine eggs, sugar and essence in small bowl, beat with electric mixer until thick and creamy. Lightly fold in sifted flour, almonds and chocolate. Pour mixture into prepared pan, bake in moderate oven for about 25 minutes or until just firm. Turn onto wire rack to cool.

Split cold cake into 2 layers. Cover base of 20cm springform tin with foil, lightly grease side of tin with oil. Place 1 cake layer into tin, pour mousse over cake, top with remaining layer of cake. Cover with plastic wrap, refrigerate for 4 hours.

Run a metal spatula around edge of cake, remove cake from tin. Dust cake with sifted icing sugar, decorate with strawberries. Serve with cream.

Chocolate Mousse: Heat cream in small saucepan, remove from heat. Add chocolate and essence, stir until chocolate is melted. Sprinkle gelatine over water, dissolve over hot water (or microwave on HIGH for about 20 seconds). Stir into chocolate mixture; transfer to large bowl.

Beat egg whites in small bowl with electric mixer until soft peaks form, gradually add sugar; beat until dissolved. Fold egg white mixture into chocolate mixture in 2 batches.

ABOVE: Date and Chocolate Torte.
RIGHT: Chocolate Mousse Sponge.

China: Incorporated Agencies; tiles: Northbridge Ceramic & Marble Centre (above). China: Noritake (right)

GLAZED CHOCOLATE APRICOT ROLL

Unglazed roll can be kept, covered, for a day in refrigerator. Grand Marnier is an orange-flavoured liqueur. Recipe unsuitable to freeze or microwave.

4 eggs
½ cup castor sugar
¼ cup plain flour
¼ cup self-raising flour
60g dark chocolate, melted
2 tablespoons boiling water
¼ teaspoon bicarbonate of soda
2 tablespoons icing sugar
APRICOT CREAM FILLING
¾ cup thickened cream
1 tablespoon Grand Marnier
425g can apricot halves, drained, chopped
GLAZE
⅓ cup light corn syrup
30g unsalted butter
2 tablespoons water
100g dark chocolate, chopped

Grease 25cm x 30cm Swiss roll pan, cover base with paper, grease paper. Beat eggs in medium bowl with electric mixer until thick and creamy, gradually add sugar, beat until dissolved after each addition. Transfer to large bowl, fold in sifted flours, then combined chocolate, water and soda.

Spread mixture into prepared pan, bake in moderate oven for about 12 minutes or until firm. Turn roll immediately onto sheet of greaseproof paper which has been sprinkled evenly with sifted icing sugar. Remove lining paper, trim edges, roll gently from narrow end, using sugared paper to lift cake and guide roll. Stand 5 minutes, unroll, cool to room temperature. Spread filling evenly over cake, roll again. Refrigerate roll for at least 1 hour before coating with warm glaze. Place roll on wire rack over tray. Pour warm glaze over roll. Stand at room temperature until glaze is set. Decorate roll with extra apricots and chocolate curls, if desired (see glossary).

Apricot Cream Filling: Beat cream and liqueur until soft peaks form, fold apricots into mixture.

Glaze: Combine corn syrup, butter and water in saucepan, stir constantly over heat, without boiling, until smooth; remove from heat. Stir in chocolate, stir until melted; allow to cool to warm before using.

LEFT: Glazed Chocolate Apricot Roll.
ABOVE, RIGHT: Choc-Chip Orange Sour Cream Cake.

Plate: Village Living; tray: Keyhole Furniture (left). Cake stand: Saywell (above, right)

CHOC-CHIP ORANGE SOUR CREAM CAKE

Cake can be made up to 4 days ahead; keep, covered, in refrigerator. Recipe unsuitable to freeze or microwave.

185g butter
2 teaspoons grated orange rind
1¼ cups castor sugar
4 eggs
100g Choc Bits
¾ cup sour cream
2 cups plain flour
½ teaspoon bicarbonate of soda
ORANGE SYRUP
½ cup sugar
¼ cup orange juice

Grease 20cm baba pan, sprinkle with flour, shake out excess flour. Combine butter, rind and sugar in medium bowl, beat with electric mixer until light and fluffy; beat in eggs 1 at a time, beat until combined. Fold in Choc Bits and sour cream, then sifted flour and soda.

Spread into prepared pan, bake in moderately slow oven for about 55 minutes or until firm. Stand 5 minutes before turning onto wire rack. Place tray underneath rack, pour hot syrup evenly over hot cake.

Orange Syrup: Combine sugar and juice in saucepan, stir over heat, without boiling, until sugar dissolves; bring to boil, remove from heat.

CHOCOLATE CHIFFON CAKE

Cake can be made a day ahead; keep, covered, in refrigerator. Plain cake can be frozen for 2 months. Recipe unsuitable to microwave.

½ cup cocoa
¾ cup boiling water
2 cups self-raising flour
1½ cups castor sugar
7 eggs, separated
½ cup oil
1 teaspoon vanilla essence
50g dark chocolate, melted
BRANDIED BUTTER CREAM
125g butter
2 cups icing sugar
2 tablespoons cocoa
2 tablespoons brandy
CHOCOLATE GLAZE
150g dark chocolate, melted
30g butter, melted

WALNUT PRALINE
1 cup sugar
½ cup walnuts
60g dark chocolate, chopped

Grease deep 23cm round cake pan, cover base with paper, grease paper. Blend cocoa with boiling water in small bowl; cool. Sift flour and sugar into large bowl, pour in cocoa mixture, egg yolks, oil and essence. Beat with electric mixer until smooth and mixture is changed in colour. Beat egg whites in large bowl with electric mixer until soft peaks form, fold into chocolate mixture in 4 batches.

Pour into prepared pan, bake in moderately slow oven for about 1 hour or until firm. Stand 5 minutes before turning onto wire rack to cool.

Split cold cake into 3 layers, join layers with some of the butter cream. Spread cake evenly with chocolate glaze. Decorate with remaining butter cream, walnut praline and chocolate.

Brandied Butter Cream: Cream butter in small bowl with electric mixer until as white as possible, beat in sifted icing sugar and cocoa, then brandy.

Chocolate Glaze: Stir chocolate and butter in small bowl until smooth.

Walnut Praline: Place sugar in heavy-based frying pan, cook over heat, without stirring, until sugar is melted and golden brown. Add nuts, pour onto greased oven tray; cool. Blend or process praline with chocolate until finely chopped. Left-over praline can be stored in an airtight container in refrigerator (see glossary).

ABOVE: Chocolate Chiffon Cake.

Glass platter: Studio-Haus; tiles: Pazotti

DOUBLE CHOCOLATE HAZELNUT TORTE

Tia Maria and Kahlua are coffee-flavoured liqueurs. Torte can be made up to 2 days in advance; keep, covered in refrigerator. Recipe unsuitable to freeze or microwave.

4 eggs, separated
⅜ cup castor sugar
1½ cups (160g) packaged ground hazelnuts
¼ cup plain flour
125g white chocolate, melted
125g dark chocolate, melted
2 x 300ml cartons thickened cream
1½ tablespoons gelatine
¼ cup water
2 teaspoons white rum
2 teaspoons Tia Maria or Kahlua

Grease bases of 3 x 23cm springform tins, cover bases with paper, grease paper. Bases can be cooked 1 at a time. Beat 3 of the egg whites in small bowl with electric mixer until soft peaks form, gradually add sugar, beat until dissolved between each addition. Fold in combined hazelnuts and sifted flour. Spread mixture evenly over prepared bases. Bake in moderately slow oven for about 25 minutes or until firm. Stand 5 minutes before removing from bases with spatula.

Place warm white chocolate in large bowl, stir in 2 egg yolks. Place warm dark chocolate in another large bowl, stir in 2 egg yolks. Whip cream in another bowl, fold half the cream into each chocolate mixture.

Sprinkle gelatine over water, dissolve over hot water (or microwave on HIGH for about 30 seconds), cool slightly, do not allow to set. Stir half into each chocolate mixture. Fold rum into white chocolate mixture and liqueur into dark chocolate mixture. Beat remaining egg white in small bowl until soft peaks form, fold into each chocolate mixture. Spread 40cm strip plastic wrap over base of springform tin, top with 1 layer of meringue, flat side down. Place springform side around base, fit plastic wrap so it lines inside of pan completely. Pour in white chocolate mixture, cover with another layer of meringue. Pour in dark chocolate mixture, top with remaining meringue. Cover, refrigerate until set.

Release springform side from tin, remove torte, carefully pull plastic wrap away from side. Invert torte onto serving plate, remove base and plastic wrap. Spread with extra whipped cream, decorate with cracked toffee and chocolate curls (see glossary).

BELOW: Double Chocolate Hazelnut Torte.

Dish: Royal Copenhagen

CARAMEL HAZELNUT TORTE

This flourless cake is best prepared a day ahead; keep, covered, in refrigerator. Plain cake can be frozen for 2 months. This recipe is unsuitable to microwave.

185g unsalted butter
2 teaspoons grated orange rind
¾ cup brown sugar, firmly packed
6 eggs, separated
185g dark chocolate, melted
1½ cups (165g) packaged ground hazelnuts
300ml carton thickened cream
WHITE CHOCOLATE CREAM
⅓ cup cream
200g white chocolate, chopped

Grease 23cm springform tin, cover base with paper, grease paper. Combine butter, rind and sugar in small bowl, beat with electric mixer until light and creamy; beat in egg yolks, beat until combined. Transfer to large bowl, stir in cooled chocolate, then hazelnuts.

Beat egg whites in medium bowl with electric mixer until soft peaks form, lightly fold into chocolate mixture in 2 batches.

Spread mixture evenly into prepared tin, bake in moderate oven for 20 minutes; reduce heat to moderately slow, bake further 45 minutes or until firm, cool in tin. Remove springform side, lift cake onto serving plate.

Spread top of cake with white chocolate cream. Beat cream until soft peaks form, spread top and side of cake with cream.

White Chocolate Cream: Place cream in small saucepan, bring to boil, remove from heat, add chocolate, stir until smooth; cool. Refrigerate for about 30 minutes or until mixture is thick and spreadable.

ALMOND MOCHA TORTE WITH CHOCOLATE LACE

Tia Maria and Kahlua are coffee-flavoured liqueurs. Torte is best prepared a day ahead. Plain cake can be frozen for up to 2 months. Recipe unsuitable to microwave.

SPONGE
3 eggs
½ cup castor sugar
¾ cup self-raising flour
¼ cup cocoa
1 tablespoon dry instant coffee
2 tablespoons hot water
⅓ cup packaged ground almonds
COFFEE SYRUP
¼ cup water
2 tablespoons sugar
1 tablespoon Tia Maria or Kahlua
MOCHA FILLING
185g unsalted butter
3 cups icing sugar

1½ teaspoons dry instant coffee
¼ cup cocoa
⅓ cup hot water
PRALINE
¼ cup sugar
2 tablespoons water
⅓ cup almonds
CHOCOLATE LACE
90g Choc Melts, melted

Sponge: Grease deep 20cm round cake pan, cover base with paper, grease paper. Beat eggs in small bowl with electric mixer until thick and creamy. Add sugar gradually, beating until dissolved. Transfer mixture to large bowl, fold in sifted flour and cocoa, then stir in combined coffee and water and almonds.

Spread into prepared pan, bake in moderate oven for about 35 minutes or until firm. Turn onto wire rack to cool.

Cut cake into 4 layers, brush 1 layer with a little of the syrup; place on serving plate. Reserve ⅓ of the filling. Spread cake with a layer of the remaining filling; repeat layering until cake, syrup and filling are used; refrigerate 1 hour.

Spread side of cake with a thin layer of reserved filling, press praline around side of cake. Spread a thin layer of filling on top of cake; mark cake into 10 wedges. Place remaining filling into piping bag fitted with small star tube, pipe filling along each marked wedge, top with chocolate lace.

Coffee Syrup: Combine water and sugar in small saucepan, stir constantly over heat, without boiling, until sugar is dissolved; bring to boil, boil 1 minute, remove from heat; cool, add liqueur.

Mocha Filling: Beat butter and sifted icing sugar together in small bowl with electric mixer until light and fluffy. Blend coffee and cocoa in small bowl with water, gradually beat into butter mixture, beat until smooth.

Praline: Combine sugar and water in small heavy-based saucepan, stir constantly over heat, without boiling, until sugar is dissolved, then boil, without stirring, until golden brown. Add almonds, pour onto greased oven tray. When set, chop praline finely. Left-over praline can be stored in an airtight container for several months (see glossary).

Chocolate Lace: Draw 10 triangles on greaseproof or baking paper, slightly smaller than marked wedges on cake. Pipe chocolate around edges of triangles, pipe chocolate back and forth across triangles for a lacy pattern, refrigerate until set (see glossary).

LEFT: Caramel Hazelnut Torte.
ABOVE: Almond Mocha Torte with Chocolate Lace.

Plate: Limoges (left). China: Royal Copenhagen; table: Sydney Antique Centre (above)

LEMON AND NUT CHOCOLATE CAKE

Hazelnut spread, for example, Nutella, is available at supermarkets. Cake can be made a day ahead; keep, covered, in refrigerator. Plain cake can be frozen for 2 months. Recipe unsuitable to microwave.

5 eggs, separated
2 teaspoons grated lemon rind
½ cup castor sugar
100g dark chocolate, grated
1 cup plain flour
½ teaspoon ground cinnamon
1 cup packaged ground hazelnuts
60g butter, melted
¼ cup castor sugar, extra
HAZELNUT CREAM FILLING
125g butter
2 teaspoons vanilla essence
2 cups icing sugar
3 tablespoons hazelnut spread
CHOCOLATE ICING
150g dark chocolate, melted
60g butter, melted
HAZELNUT PRALINE
1 cup sugar
½ cup unroasted hazelnuts

Grease deep 20cm round cake pan, cover base with paper, grease paper. Beat egg yolks and rind in small bowl with electric mixer until thick, gradually add sugar, beat until thick and creamy.

FIG FUDGE CAKE WITH MILK CHOCOLATE ICING

Hazelnuts and breadcrumbs replace the flour in this cake. Cake will keep for 3 days, covered, in refrigerator. Plain cake can be frozen for up to 2 months. Recipe unsuitable to microwave.

¾ cup chopped dried figs
½ cup brandy
1½ cups (160g) roasted hazelnuts
¼ cup packaged breadcrumbs
125g butter
⅔ cup castor sugar
3 eggs
125g dark chocolate, melted
MILK CHOCOLATE ICING
⅓ cup sugar
100g milk chocolate, chopped
½ cup thickened cream

Combine figs and brandy in saucepan, bring to boil; boil, uncovered, until brandy is evaporated. Transfer figs to bowl, cool to room temperature.

Grease deep 20cm round cake pan, cover base with paper, grease paper. Blend or process hazelnuts and breadcrumbs until hazelnuts are finely chopped (not ground). Combine butter and sugar in small bowl, beat with electric mixer until light and fluffy; add eggs 1 at a time, beat until combined. Mixture might curdle at this stage but will reconstitute later. Stir in hazelnut and fig mixtures and cooled chocolate. Pour mixture into prepared pan, bake in moderate oven for about 45 minutes or until firm; cool in pan.

Turn cake onto serving plate, spread with milk chocolate icing. Refrigerate for several hours before serving. Decorate with toffee-dipped hazelnuts and toffee lace, if desired (see glossary).

Milk Chocolate Icing: Place sugar in small heavy-based saucepan, cook until sugar is completely melted and golden brown. Stir in chocolate and cream, stir constantly over heat, without boiling, until mixture is smooth; cool to room temperature.

Transfer mixture to large bowl, stir in chocolate and sifted flour and cinnamon, then hazelnuts and butter. Beat egg whites in medium bowl until soft peaks form, gradually add extra sugar, beat until dissolved. Fold into chocolate mixture in 2 batches.

Pour into prepared pan, bake in moderate oven for about 45 minutes or until firm. Stand few minutes before turning onto wire rack to cool. Split cake into 3 layers; sandwich together on serving plate, using two-thirds of the filling. Spread cake evenly all over with icing. Decorate with remaining filling and praline.

Hazelnut Cream Filling: Beat butter and essence in small bowl with electric mixer until as white as possible. Gradually beat in sifted icing sugar, then hazelnut spread.

Chocolate Icing: Combine chocolate and butter in small bowl, stir until smooth and spreadable.

Hazelnut Praline: Place sugar in small heavy-based frying pan, cook until sugar melts and turns golden brown. Add nuts, pour onto lightly greased oven tray; cool. When set, blend or process until finely crushed. Left-over praline can be stored in an airtight jar for several months (see glossary).

RICH MOCHA GATEAU

Cointreau is a citrus-flavoured liqueur. Cake can be prepared up to a day ahead; store, covered, in refrigerator. This recipe is unsuitable to freeze or microwave.

½ cup Cointreau
2 teaspoons grated orange rind
150g milk chocolate, melted
90g unsalted butter, melted
6 eggs, separated
¾ **cup self-raising flour**
⅓ **cup castor sugar**
RICH MOCHA FILLING
2 teaspoons dry instant coffee
2 tablespoons hot water
300g dark chocolate, melted
6 egg yolks
CHOCOLATE BUTTER CREAM
2 tablespoons dry instant coffee
¼ **cup hot water**
200g dark chocolate, melted
4 egg yolks
¼ **cup castor sugar**
185g unsalted butter, softened

Combine liqueur and rind in small bowl, stand 30 minutes, strain; reserve both rind and liqueur. Grease base and side of deep 23cm round cake pan, cover base with paper, grease paper.

Combine chocolate, butter and reserved rind in large bowl, mix well. Stir in 3 teaspoons of the reserved liqueur, egg yolks and sifted flour. Beat egg whites in large bowl with electric mixer until soft peaks form, gradually add sugar to egg whites; beat until dissolved between each addition.

Gently fold egg whites into chocolate mixture in 2 batches.

Pour into prepared pan, bake in moderate oven for about 35 minutes or until firm, stand 5 minutes before turning onto wire rack to cool.

Split cake into 3 layers. Place 1 layer onto serving plate, spread with half the mocha filling, refrigerate 15 minutes. Add another layer of cake and remaining mocha filling, then add third layer; refrigerate 30 minutes. Completely cover cake with butter cream, refrigerate 30 minutes.

Rich Mocha Filling: Combine coffee and water in large bowl, stir in cooled chocolate, then egg yolks, then ⅓ cup of the reserved liqueur. Refrigerate filling several hours or until set.

Chocolate Butter Cream: Combine coffee and water in large bowl, stir in remaining reserved liqueur and the chocolate, stir until smooth.

Beat egg yolks with sugar in small bowl with electric mixer until thick and creamy, beat in butter in several batches, beat until smooth. Gradually beat in chocolate mixture while motor is operating. Refrigerate 10 minutes or until spreadable.

ABOVE: Rich Mocha Gateau. LEFT, ABOVE: Fig Fudge Cake with Milk Chocolate Icing. LEFT: Lemon and Nut Chocolate Cake.

China: Villeroy & Boch; painting by Stephen Gill (above). China: Limoges (left)

51

THE UNBELIEVABLY RICH CHOCOLATE NUT CAKE

Cake can be made up to a week ahead; keep, covered, in refrigerator. Plain cake can be frozen for 2 months. Recipe unsuitable to microwave.

1 cup slivered almonds
1¼ cups (190g) brazil nuts, coarsely chopped
1½ cups coconut
¼ cup chopped glacé ginger
1½ cups (210g) currants
½ cup plain flour
½ cup cocoa
1 teaspoon ground cinnamon
250g dark chocolate, chopped
¼ cup honey
½ cup sweet orange marmalade
60g butter
RICH CHOCOLATE ICING
150g dark chocolate melted
30g butter, melted

Grease 20cm flan tin, cover base with paper, grease paper. Combine nuts, coconut, ginger and currants with sifted flour, cocoa and cinnamon in large bowl. Combine chocolate, honey, marmalade and butter in saucepan, stir constantly over low heat until chocolate is melted. Stir mixture into dry ingredients.

Press into prepared tin; bake in moderately slow oven for about 45 minutes or until firm; cool in tin. Turn cake onto wire rack, spread all over with icing, refrigerate until set. Serve with whipped cream, if desired.
Rich Chocolate Icing: Combine chocolate and butter in small bowl; stir until smooth.

CHOCOLATE YOGHURT CAKE WITH RED CURRANT CREAM

Cake can be made up to 2 days ahead; keep, covered, in refrigerator. Plain cake can be frozen for 2 months. Recipe unsuitable to microwave.

1¾ cups self-raising flour
2 cups castor sugar
¾ cup cocoa
2 eggs, lightly beaten
2 teaspoons dry instant coffee
¾ cup boiling water
¾ cup plain yoghurt
125g butter, melted
1 teaspoon vanilla essence
⅓ cup red currant jelly, warmed
RED CURRANT CREAM
250g unsalted butter
⅔ cup red currant jelly

Grease deep 23cm round cake pan, cover base with paper, grease paper. Combine sifted flour, sugar and cocoa in large bowl with eggs, combined coffee and water, yoghurt, butter and essence, beat with electric mixer on low speed until combined; increase speed, beat until mixture is smooth and changed in colour.

Pour mixture into prepared pan, bake in moderate oven for about 1 hour or until firm, stand 5 minutes before turning onto wire rack to cool.

Split cake into 3 layers. Sandwich layers together on serving plate using some of the red currant cream. Cover cake with remaining red currant cream; refrigerate until firm. Spread red currant jelly over cream, decorate with extra chocolate and cream, if desired.
Red Currant Cream: Place butter in small bowl, beat with electric mixer until as white as possible. Gradually beat in jelly until smooth.

ABOVE: The Unbelievably Rich Chocolate Nut Cake. RIGHT: Chocolate Yoghurt Cake with Red Currant Cream.

China and rug: Australian East India Company (above). Plate and fork: Sydney Antique Centre (right)

LAMINGTON BUTTERFLY SPONGE

Cake is best served the day it is made. Plain cake can be frozen for up to 2 months. This recipe is unsuitable to microwave.

4 eggs
⅓ cup castor sugar
100g dark chocolate, melted
¾ cup self-raising flour
¼ cup cornflour
15g butter, melted
¼ cup hot water

¼ cup strawberry jam
300ml carton thickened cream
strawberries
CHOCOLATE ICING
1½ cups icing sugar
100g dark chocolate, melted
2 teaspoons butter
¼ cup milk
¾ cup coconut, approximately

Grease deep 20cm round cake pan, cover base with paper, grease paper. Beat eggs in medium bowl with electric mixer until thick and creamy; gradually add sugar, beat until dissolved

between each addition; beat in cooled chocolate. Lightly fold in sifted flours, then combined butter and water.

Spread mixture into prepared pan; bake in moderate oven for about 35 minutes or until firm. Turn onto wire rack to cool.

Spread icing all over cake; sprinkle evenly with coconut. When icing is set cut cake into 4 layers. Sandwich 3 of the layers together with jam and a little of the whipped cream. Spread top of third layer with jam. Cut remaining layer of cake into 8 wedges; place into

CHOCOLATE BANANA CAKE

We used 2 large bananas for this recipe. Cake can be kept in an airtight container for 2 days or frozen for 2 months. This recipe is unsuitable to microwave.

125g butter
¾ cup brown sugar, firmly packed
2 eggs
1 cup mashed over-ripe banana
1½ cups self-raising flour
2 tablespoons cocoa
½ teaspoon bicarbonate of soda
¾ cup sour cream
1 teaspoon icing sugar

Grease 20cm baba or ring pan. Cream butter and sugar in small bowl with electric mixer until light and fluffy, add eggs one at a time; beat until combined. Transfer mixture to large bowl, stir in banana, then sifted flour, cocoa and soda with sour cream in 2 batches; mix well.

Spread into prepared pan, bake in moderate oven for about 45 minutes or until firm; stand 10 minutes before turning onto wire rack to cool.

Cool cake further 10 minutes, sprinkle lightly with icing sugar, serve warm with whipped cream, if desired, or cold with butter.

position, as shown, using remaining cream and strawberries to support each wedge.
Chocolate Icing: Sift icing sugar into heatproof bowl, stir in chocolate, butter and milk, stir constantly over hot water until icing is spreadable.

ABOVE: Lamington Butterfly Sponge.
RIGHT: Chocolate Banana Cake.

Glass platter: Dansab; plate: Lifestyle Imports (above). Plate: Studio Kara (right)

HAZELNUT COFFEE LOG

This cake is best made the day before required to allow layers to soften slightly. Recipe is unsuitable to freeze or microwave.

185g unsalted butter
²/₃ cup castor sugar
1¹/₄ cups plain flour
³/₄ cup packaged ground hazelnuts
300ml carton thickened cream
MILK COFFEE FILLING
60g unsalted butter
½ cup castor sugar
2 tablespoons plain flour
1³/₄ cups milk
1 tablespoon dry instant coffee
100g milk chocolate, chopped

Cream butter and sugar in medium bowl with electric mixer until light and fluffy. Stir in sifted flour and hazelnuts. Turn dough onto lightly floured surface, knead gently until smooth. Divide dough into 4 pieces, wrap each piece of dough in plastic wrap, refrigerate 30 minutes.

Roll each piece of dough between sheets of plastic wrap to 10cm x 20cm rectangle. Place dough onto 2 lightly greased oven trays. Bake in moderate oven for about 15 minutes or until just firm around the edges.

While layers are still warm, lift from trays to board and trim edges to make the layers all the same size. Return layers to trays to cool completely. Sandwich hazelnut layers together with the filling, cover, refrigerate overnight.

Next day, cover cake with whipped cream, decorate with chocolate curls, if desired (see glossary).

Milk Coffee Filling: Melt butter in small saucepan, stir in sugar and flour, stir over heat for 1 minute. Gradually stir in milk, coffee and chocolate, stir constantly over heat until mixture boils and thickens. Transfer to bowl, cover with plastic wrap, cool, refrigerate 30 minutes before using.

CHOCOLATE MARSALA CAKE

Cake can be kept in refrigerator in airtight container for 2 days; uniced cake can be frozen for 2 months. This recipe is unsuitable to microwave.

125g butter
3 eggs
1¹/₃ cups castor sugar
1³/₄ cups self-raising flour
¹/₃ cup cocoa
½ teaspoon bicarbonate of soda
³/₄ cup milk
2 tablespoons marsala
½ cup thickened cream
1 teaspoon marsala, extra
1 teaspoon cocoa, extra

Grease deep 19cm square cake pan, cover base with paper, grease paper. Combine butter, eggs, sugar, sifted flour, cocoa and soda and milk in large bowl, beat on low speed with electric mixer until ingredients are combined. Increase speed to medium, beat for about 3 minutes or until mixture is smooth and changed in colour.

Spread into prepared pan; bake in moderate oven for about 1¹/₄ hours or until firm. Brush hot cake with marsala; stand 5 minutes before turning onto wire rack to cool.

Serve cake spread with combined whipped cream and extra marsala, sprinkle with extra sifted cocoa.

ABOVE: Hazelnut Coffee Log. RIGHT: Chocolate Marsala Cake.

Plate: Mikasa (above). Plate: Sydney Antique Centre (right)

56

CHOCOLATE APPLE CAKE WITH ORANGE FROSTING

Cake can be kept in an airtight container for 2 days; unfrosted cake can be frozen for 2 months. Recipe unsuitable to microwave.

2¼ cups self-raising flour
¼ cup cocoa
1 teaspoon ground cinnamon
1 cup brown sugar, firmly packed
⅓ cup chopped raisins
125g butter, melted
2 eggs, lightly beaten
⅔ cup milk
1 medium apple, grated
50g dark chocolate, melted
ORANGE FROSTING
60g butter
1 teaspoon coarsely grated
**   orange rind**
1½ cups icing sugar
2 tablespoons orange juice,
**   approximately**

Grease deep 23cm round cake pan, cover base with paper, grease paper. Combine sifted flour, cocoa and cinnamon in large bowl; add sugar, raisins, butter, eggs, milk and apple, stir until well combined.

Pour into prepared pan, bake in moderate oven for about 1¼ hours or until firm. Stand 10 minutes before turning onto wire rack to cool. Top with frosting and pipe or drizzle with dark chocolate.

Orange Frosting: Combine butter and rind in small bowl, beat with electric mixer until light and creamy. Gradually add sifted icing sugar and enough orange juice to make spreadable.

SUGAR 'N' SPICE CAKE

Cake can be prepared up to 4 days ahead; keep, covered, in refrigerator. Cake can be frozen for 2 months. Recipe unsuitable to microwave.

125g butter
1¼ cups brown sugar, firmly packed
3 eggs
1 cup self-raising flour
¼ cup cocoa
1 teaspoon ground cinnamon
½ teaspoon ground ginger
½ teaspoon ground nutmeg
1 cup cream
1 tablespoon icing sugar

Grease 23cm square slab pan, cover base with paper, grease paper. Cream butter and sugar in small bowl with electric mixer until light and fluffy; beat in eggs 1 at a time, beat until combined. Transfer mixture to large bowl, fold in sifted flour, cocoa and spices and cream in 2 batches, stir until smooth.

Spread into prepared pan, bake in moderately slow oven for about 1¼ hours or until firm. Stand 5 minutes before turning onto wire rack to cool. Serve dusted with sifted icing sugar.

CHOCOLATE HONEY SPONGE

Cake can be made a day ahead; keep, covered, in refrigerator. Plain cake can be frozen for 2 months. Recipe unsuitable to microwave.

3 eggs
½ cup castor sugar
¼ cup plain flour
¼ cup self-raising flour
2 tablespoons cornflour
2 tablespoons cocoa
1 tablespoon honey, warmed
2 tablespoons honey, warmed, extra
2 tablespoons brandy
2 x 300ml cartons thickened cream
50g dark chocolate, grated

Grease deep 20cm round cake pan, cover base with paper, grease paper. Beat eggs in small bowl with electric mixer until thick and creamy, gradually add sugar; beat until dissolved between each addition. Transfer mixture to large bowl, fold in sifted flours and cocoa then honey.

Spread mixture into prepared pan; bake in moderate oven for about 35 minutes or until firm. Turn onto wire rack to cool.

Split cold cake into 3 layers, brush each layer with combined extra honey and brandy. Whip cream until firm peaks form; fold in chocolate. Join cake layers with half the cream mixture, cover cake with remaining cream mixture. Decorate with chocolate triangles (see glossary).

ABOVE: Chocolate Apple Cake with Orange Frosting. RIGHT, ABOVE: Chocolate Honey Sponge. RIGHT: Sugar 'n' Spice Cake.

Glass Platter: Inini (above). Plate: Royal Copenhagen; washstand in background: Sydney Antique Centre (right, above). China and cake fork: Sydney Antique Centre (right)

PASSIONFRUIT SATIN CAKE

You will need about 12 passionfruit for this recipe; strain pulp to obtain juice required. Cake is best made a day ahead; keep, covered, in refrigerator. Recipe unsuitable to freeze or microwave.

125g White Melts, melted
½ cup warm water
125g butter
1 cup castor sugar
2 eggs
½ cup sour cream
1¼ cups plain flour
½ cup self-raising flour
100g white chocolate, coarsely grated
PASSIONFRUIT SYRUP
½ cup water
¼ cup sugar
2 tablespoons passionfruit juice
PASSIONFRUIT FILLING
¼ cup water
½ cup sugar
2 tablespoons passionfruit juice
1½ tablespoons passionfruit seeds
250g unsalted butter

Grease 2 x 20cm springform tin bases, cover bases with paper, grease paper. Combine White Melts and water in small bowl, stir until smooth; cool to room temperature.

Combine butter and sugar in small bowl, beat with electric mixer until light and fluffy. Add eggs one at a time, beat until combined; beat in chocolate mixture. Transfer to large bowl.

Fold in sour cream and sifted flours in 2 batches. Divide mixture into 8 portions. Spread 1 portion into each of the prepared tins. Bake in moderate oven for about 10 minutes or until lightly browned and firm. Cool cake layers on wire racks. Repeat with remaining cake mixture.

Place 1 layer of cake on serving plate, brush with syrup, spread with a thin layer of filling. Repeat with remaining cake, syrup and filling. Spread remaining filling all over cake, press grated chocolate around side; decorate with chocolate curls (see glossary), if desired.

Passionfruit Syrup: Combine water and sugar in small saucepan; stir constantly over heat, without boiling, until sugar is dissolved. Bring to boil, boil 1 minute, remove from heat, cool; add passionfruit juice.

Passionfruit Filling: Combine water and sugar in small saucepan, stir constantly over heat, without boiling, until sugar is dissolved; remove from heat, cool, add juice and seeds. Beat butter in small bowl with electric mixer until as white as possible; gradually add cold syrup, while the motor is operating.

RIGHT: Passionfruit Satin Cake.

CHOCONUT FIESTA CAKE

Frosted cake will keep for up to 3 days in an airtight container; unfrosted cake can be frozen for 2 months. Recipe unsuitable to microwave.

125g butter
½ teaspoon coconut essence
1 cup castor sugar
2 eggs
½ cup coconut
1½ cups self-raising flour
⅓ cup cocoa
300g carton sour cream
⅔ cup milk
COCONUT FROSTING
2 cups icing sugar
1⅓ cups coconut
2 egg whites, lightly beaten

Grease deep 23cm round cake pan, cover base with paper, grease paper. Cream butter, essence and sugar in small bowl with electric mixer until light and fluffy; beat in eggs 1 at a time, beat until combined. Transfer mixture to large bowl, stir in coconut, sifted flour and cocoa and combined cream and milk in 2 batches, stir until smooth.

Pour mixture into prepared pan, bake in moderate oven for about 1 hour or until firm. Stand 5 minutes before turning onto wire rack to cool. Top with frosting when cold.

Coconut Frosting: Combine sifted icing sugar in bowl with coconut, stir in egg whites.

BELOW: Choconut Fiesta Cake.

Plate: Lynne Phillips Country Collection

BRANDIED WALNUT SPONGE

Cake can be made up to 2 days ahead; keep, covered, in refrigerator. Recipe unsuitable to freeze or microwave.

3 cups (360g) walnuts
½ cup self-raising flour
5 eggs, separated
1 teaspoon vanilla essence
1 cup castor sugar
2 tablespoons icing sugar
½ cup red currant jelly, warmed
⅓ cup walnuts, finely chopped, extra
75g milk chocolate, grated
75g dark chocolate, grated
DARK CHOCOLATE CREAM
1⅓ cups cream
200g dark chocolate, chopped
2 tablespoons brandy
MILK CHOCOLATE CREAM
⅔ cup cream
100g milk chocolate, chopped
1 tablespoon brandy

WHITE CHOCOLATE CREAM
⅔ cup cream
100g white chocolate, chopped
1 tablespoon brandy
TOPPING
3 teaspoons gelatine
¼ cup water
¼ cup red currant jelly
1 tablespoon brandy

Lightly grease 2 deep 23cm round cake pans, cover bases with paper, grease paper. Blend or process walnuts until finely chopped, combine in large bowl with sifted flour.

Beat egg yolks and essence in small bowl, beat with electric mixer until thick and creamy; gradually add castor sugar, beat until dissolved between each addition.

Beat egg whites in medium bowl with electric mixer until soft peaks form, add sifted icing sugar; beat until combined. Stir egg yolk mixture into

walnut mixture, then egg white mixture into walnut mixture in 2 batches.

Spread mixture evenly into prepared pans; bake in moderate oven for about 35 minutes or until firm and dry. Stand 5 minutes before turning onto wire rack to cool.

Split cold cakes in half. Place plastic wrap over base of springform tin; allow enough to line side. Onto base, place layer of sponge, flat side down.

Place springform side around base, fit plastic wrap so it lines inside of tin completely. Sandwich layers, using jelly and the 3 chocolate creams. Cover, refrigerate cake several hours or overnight.

Release springform side from tin, remove cake, carefully pull plastic wrap away from side, invert cake onto serving plate. Remove base and plastic, spread side with reserved dark chocolate cream. Combine extra

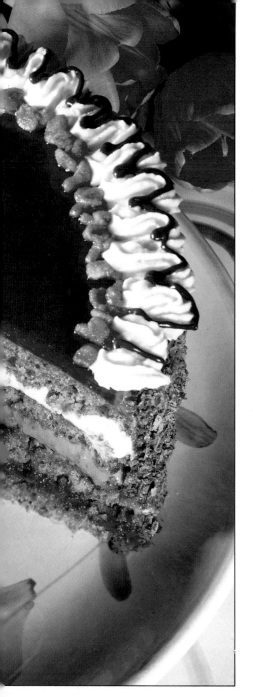

CHOCOLATE TREASURE CAKE

Cake can be made up to 2 days ahead; keep, covered, in refrigerator. Recipe unsuitable to freeze or microwave.

185g butter
1 teaspoon vanilla essence
1¾ cups castor sugar
2 eggs
2¼ cups self-raising flour
⅓ cup cocoa
1½ cups buttermilk
250g White Melts, melted
125g butter, melted, extra
CHOCOLATE CREAM
⅔ cup thickened cream
150g white chocolate, chopped
300ml carton thickened cream, extra

Grease deep 23cm round cake pan, cover base with paper, grease paper. Cream butter, essence and sugar in large bowl with electric mixer until light and fluffy; beat in eggs 1 at a time, beat until combined. Stir in sifted flour and cocoa and buttermilk in 2 batches. Spread mixture into prepared pan; bake in moderate oven for about 1 hour or until firm. Stand 5 minutes before turning onto wire rack to cool.

Using round handle of wooden spoon, push handle into cake to make tunnels about 3cm apart; do this in concentric circles.

Combine White Melts and extra butter in small bowl; stir until smooth, cool until thick. Place mixture into piping bag fitted with plain tube, pipe mixture into tunnels. Cover cake with chocolate cream. Decorate with chocolate curls (see glossary) and strawberries, if desired.

Chocolate Cream: Bring cream to boil in small saucepan, add chocolate, remove from heat, stir until smooth; cool to room temperature. Combine extra cream and chocolate mixture in small bowl, beat with electric mixer until firm peaks form.

BELOW: Chocolate Treasure Cake.

Plate: Dansab

walnuts, milk chocolate and dark chocolate in bowl, mix well, press onto side of cake. Pour topping carefully onto cake; refrigerate for 1 hour.

Dark Chocolate Cream: Bring cream to boil in saucepan, remove from heat, stir in chocolate and brandy, stir until smooth. Pour into bowl, refrigerate until beginning to set; beat until spreadable. Reserve half the mixture for side of cake.

Milk Chocolate Cream: Prepare as for dark chocolate cream.

White Chocolate Cream: Prepare as for dark chocolate cream.

Topping: Sprinkle gelatine over water in small heatproof bowl, dissolve over hot water. Add jelly and brandy, stir until smooth; stand until pourable.

ABOVE: Brandied Walnut Sponge.

Plates, tiles, napkin holder: Zuhause.

LEMON CHEESECAKE WITH CHOCOLATE GLAZE

Cheesecake can be made up to 3 days ahead; keep, covered, in refrigerator. Unglazed cheesecake can be frozen for up to a month. This recipe is unsuitable to microwave.

1 cup plain uniced chocolate biscuit crumbs
90g butter, melted
LEMON CREAM CHEESE FILLING
½ cup cream
150g White Melts, melted
500g packaged cream cheese, softened
1 cup castor sugar
3 eggs
2 teaspoons grated lemon rind
¼ cup lemon juice
CHOCOLATE GLAZE
200g dark chocolate, melted
2 tablespoons light corn syrup
60g unsalted butter, melted
Lightly grease 20cm round springform tin, cover base with foil, grease foil.

CHOCOLATE FUDGE SAUCE

Sauce will keep, covered, in refrigerator for 2 weeks. Recipe unsuitable to freeze or microwave.

½ cup cream
¼ cup castor sugar
2 teaspoons cornflour
2 teaspoons water
125g dark chocolate, chopped
2 tablespoons brandy

Combine cream and sugar in saucepan, stir constantly over heat, without boiling, until sugar is dissolved. Stir in blended cornflour and water, stir constantly over heat until mixture boils and thickens. Remove from heat, add chocolate and brandy, stir until smooth. Serve hot, warm or cold over ice-cream.

Makes about 1¾ cups.

ABOVE: Chocolate Fudge Sauce.
RIGHT: Lemon Cheesecake with Chocolate Glaze.

Bowl & scarf: Studio Kara (above)

64

Combine biscuit crumbs and butter in bowl. Press evenly over base of prepared tin, refrigerate while preparing filling.

Pour filling into tin, bake in moderate oven for about 50 minutes or until just firm in centre; cool in oven with door ajar. Remove cheesecake from tin; refrigerate 1 hour. Place cheesecake on wire rack over tray. Spread warm topping all over cheesecake, refrigerate until set. Decorate with crystallised lemon peel strands, if desired (see glossary).

Lemon Cream Cheese Filling: Combine cream and White Melts in small bowl, stir until smooth. Beat cheese and sugar in medium bowl with electric mixer until light and fluffy. Beat in chocolate mixture gradually while motor is operating. Beat in eggs 1 at a time, then lemon rind and juice; beat until combined.

Chocolate Glaze: Combine chocolate, corn syrup and butter in a bowl, stir until smooth, glossy and pourable.

Desserts

Pursue your craving for chocolate with desserts! But ours are more than desserts: they are sweet sensations from the first glimpse to the last morsel. We have included a blissful selection of tastes and textures to delight all fancies.

FROZEN CHOCOLATE AND COCONUT SOUFFLES

Soufflés can be made up to 3 days ahead; keep, covered, in freezer. Stand at room temperature 10 minutes before serving.

¼ cup cocoa
2 teaspoons plain flour
⅓ cup castor sugar
¾ cup milk
2 eggs, separated
60g white chocolate, melted
200ml can coconut cream
2 tablespoons castor sugar, extra
300ml carton thickened cream

Place collar of foil around each of 6 dishes (½ cup capacity), secure with string. Combine sifted cocoa and flour with sugar in saucepan, gradually stir in milk. Stir constantly over heat until mixture boils and thickens slightly. Remove from heat, quickly stir in lightly beaten egg yolks, transfer to medium bowl, cover with plastic wrap, cool to room temperature.

Combine white chocolate and coconut cream in large bowl; mix well. Beat egg whites in small bowl with electric mixer until soft peaks form, gradually add extra sugar; beat until dissolved. Beat cream in bowl until soft peaks form.

Gently fold half the egg white mixture and half the cream into cocoa mixture, then fold remaining egg white mixture and cream into white chocolate mixture. Add cocoa mixture, swirl mixtures together with skewer. Carefully spoon mixture into prepared dishes. Freeze soufflés for several hours or until just firm. Remove collars, decorate with extra whipped cream, chocolate curls (see glossary) and fruit, if desired.

Serves 6.

CREPES WITH FUDGE AND ORANGE SAUCES

Grand Marnier is an orange-flavoured liqueur. You will need a 300ml carton cream for this recipe. Filled crêpes can be prepared up to a day ahead; keep, covered, in refrigerator. Make sauces on day of serving. Recipe unsuitable to freeze or microwave.

CREPES
⅓ cup plain flour
2 eggs, lightly beaten
1 tablespoon oil
¾ cup milk
½ cup apricot jam, sieved
1 tablespoon Grand Marnier

LEFT: Frozen Chocolate and Coconut Soufflés. RIGHT, ABOVE: Crêpes with Fudge and Orange Sauces.

Tray: Lifestyle Imports (left). Plate: Limoges: table: Kerry Trollope Antiques (right, above)

FUDGE SAUCE
½ cup sweetened condensed milk
⅔ cup cream
100g dark chocolate, chopped
ORANGE LIQUEUR SAUCE
4 egg yolks
¼ cup sugar
1 cup milk
½ cup cream
1 tablespoon Grand Marnier

Crêpes: Sift flour into bowl, make well in centre, gradually stir in eggs, oil and milk, beat until batter is smooth, cover, refrigerate 30 minutes.

Pour 2 tablespoons batter into hot greased crêpe pan, cook until golden brown. Turn crêpe, cook other side.

Repeat with remaining batter. Spread combined jam and liqueur over crêpes, fold into triangles. Serve crêpês with both sauces.

Fudge Sauce: Combine condensed milk, cream and chocolate in small saucepan, stir constantly over low heat, without boiling, until smooth.

Orange Liqueur Sauce: Combine egg yolks and sugar in small bowl, whisk until pale in colour. Heat milk and cream in saucepan, gradually whisk milk into egg mixture, return mixture to saucepan. Stir constantly over low heat with a wooden spoon until sauce thickens slightly; do not boil. Add liqueur; cool.

SAUCY CHOCOLATE ALMOND DESSERTS

Amaretto is an almond-flavoured liqueur. Dessert should be made just before serving. Recipe unsuitable to freeze or microwave.

¾ cup self-raising flour
2 tablespoons cocoa
½ cup packaged ground almonds
⅓ cup castor sugar
½ cup milk
90g dark chocolate, melted
60g unsalted butter, melted
¾ cup brown sugar, firmly packed
2 tablespoons cocoa, extra
1½ cups boiling water
1 tablespoon icing sugar
LIQUEUR CREAM
300ml carton thickened cream
1 tablespoon castor sugar
1 tablespoon Amaretto

Sift flour and cocoa into medium bowl, stir in almonds, sugar, milk, chocolate and butter. Spread mixture evenly over bases of 6 greased ovenproof dishes (1 cup capacity); stand dishes on oven tray. Sprinkle sifted combined brown sugar and extra cocoa evenly over cake mixture. Pour boiling water evenly over brown sugar and cocoa. Bake in moderate oven for about 30 minutes or until firm and crusty. Sprinkle with sifted icing sugar. Serve desserts with liqueur cream.

Liqueur Cream: Beat cream and sugar in small bowl until thick, add liqueur, beat until soft peaks form.
Serves 6.

CHOCOLATE ZABAGLIONE

Zabaglione should be made just before serving. This recipe is unsuitable to freeze or microwave.

4 egg yolks
⅓ cup castor sugar
⅓ cup marsala
3 teaspoons cocoa

Combine egg yolks and sugar in top of double saucepan (or in heatproof bowl), beat over simmering water with rotary beater or electric mixer until thick and creamy; do not allow water to touch base of top saucepan or bowl. Gradually beat in combined marsala and sifted cocoa, beat constantly over simmering water for further 5 minutes or until mixture is thick and creamy. Spoon mixture into 4 serving glasses.
Serves 4.

RIGHT: Saucy Chocolate Almond Desserts. BELOW: Chocolate Zabaglione.

Plate: Royal Copenhagen (right). Glasses: Studio-Haus (below)

68

CHOCOLATE TOFFEE PUFFS

Unfilled puffs can be frozen for up to 2 months. Filling can be prepared up to 3 days ahead; keep, covered, in refrigerator. Fill and dip puffs as close to serving time as possible. Recipe unsuitable to microwave.

CHOUX PASTRY
75g butter, chopped
1 cup water
1 cup plain flour
4 eggs
ORANGE CHOCOLATE FILLING
2 egg yolks
¼ cup castor sugar
1 cup milk
1 tablespoon plain flour
1 tablespoon cornflour
1 teaspoon grated orange rind
120g white chocolate, grated
300ml carton thickened cream
CHOCOLATE TOFFEE
1 cup sugar
½ cup water
60g Choc Melts, finely chopped

Choux Pastry: Combine butter and water in saucepan, bring to boil. When butter is melted and water boiling, add sifted flour all at once; stir vigorously over heat until mixture leaves sides of saucepan and forms a smooth ball.

Transfer mixture to small bowl of electric mixer, add eggs 1 at a time, beating well between each addition. Spoon mixture into piping bag fitted with plain tube. Pipe mounds of pastry about 2cm diameter on lightly greased oven trays, about 5cm apart.

Bake in hot oven for 10 minutes, reduce heat to moderate, bake further 15 minutes or until puffs are lightly browned and crisp.

Make a small slit in side of each puff to allow steam to escape, return to moderate oven for about 10 minutes or until dry and crisp; cool.

Place filling in piping bag fitted with a small plain tube. Pierce base of puffs with tube and fill with filling. Dip tops of puffs carefully into chocolate toffee. Arrange puffs as shown; decorate with chocolate leaves (see glossary).

Orange Chocolate Filling: Combine egg yolks, sugar, ¼ cup of the milk and flours in medium bowl, stir until smooth. Bring remaining milk and rind to boil in saucepan. Gradually stir into egg mixture, stir until smooth.

Return mixture to saucepan, stir constantly over heat until mixture boils and thickens. Remove from heat; stir in chocolate; cover, cool to room temperature. Beat cream until soft

peaks form, fold into filling.

Chocolate Toffee: Combine sugar and water in saucepan. Stir constantly over heat, without boiling, until sugar is dissolved. Bring to boil, boil rapidly, without stirring, until toffee is golden brown; remove from heat, allow bubbles to subside. Place Choc Melts in heatproof bowl, slowly stir in toffee, stir gently until all the toffee is incorporated. Do not stir vigorously as toffee could crystallise.

MINTED CHOCOLATE FLAN

Flan can be made 2 days ahead, keep, covered, in refrigerator. Recipe unsuitable to freeze.

NUTTY BISCUIT BASE
1 cup packaged ground
   hazelnuts
125g butter, melted
2 cups (250g) plain uniced chocolate
   biscuit crumbs
MINTED CHOCOLATE FILLING
2 eggs
½ cup castor sugar
⅓ cup cornflour
1½ cups milk

200g dark chocolate, chopped
3 teaspoons gelatine
2 tablespoons water
peppermint essence
300ml carton thickened cream

Nutty Biscuit Base: Combine hazelnuts, butter and crumbs in bowl, mix well; press mixture evenly over base and side of 23cm flan tin (with removable base), refrigerate 30 minutes. Spoon filling into tin, smooth top, refrigerate several hours before serving. Decorate with extra whipped cream, strawberries and chocolate curls, if desired (see glossary).

Minted Chocolate Filling: Beat eggs and sugar in small bowl with electric mixer until thick and creamy, stir in blended cornflour and milk. Pour mixture into saucepan, stir constantly over heat until mixture boils and thickens. Remove from heat, add chocolate, stir until melted.

Sprinkle gelatine over water, dissolve over hot water. Add to chocolate mixture, cool to room temperature; stir in essence to taste. Beat cream until soft peaks form, fold into chocolate mixture.

ABOVE RIGHT: Chocolate Toffee Puffs.
RIGHT: Minted Chocolate Flan.

China: Villeroy & Boch; table in background: Suko (right)

70

CHUNKY CHOCOLATE PECAN FLAN

Flan can be made up to 2 days ahead; keep, covered, in refrigerator. Flan can be frozen for up to a month. Recipe unsuitable to microwave.

PASTRY
155g unsalted butter
3 eggs
¾ cup castor sugar
2½ cups plain flour

FRUIT MINCE FILLING
410g jar fruit mince
1 tablespoon brandy
2 teaspoons grated lemon rind
1 teaspoon grated orange rind

CHOCOLATE PECAN TOPPING
1 egg
¼ cup castor sugar
60g butter, melted
¼ cup plain flour
½ cup Choc Bits
½ cup pecans, chopped

Pastry: Combine butter, eggs and sugar in processor, process until just combined. Add flour to mixture, process until mixture forms a dough. Turn dough onto lightly floured surface, knead lightly until smooth, cover, refrigerate 30 minutes.

Roll dough between greaseproof paper until it is large enough to line 23cm flan tin, trim edges, cover with greaseproof paper, fill with dried beans or rice; bake in moderately hot oven for 7 minutes. Remove paper and beans, bake further 7 minutes.

Spread filling over base, spread topping over filling. Bake in moderate oven for 45 minutes or until firm; cool to room temperature. Decorate with piped chocolate, chocolate shapes (see glossary) and strawberries.

Fruit Mince Filling: Combine all ingredients in bowl; mix well.

Chocolate Pecan Topping: Combine egg, sugar, butter and sifted flour in small bowl, beat with electric mixer until smooth and combined; stir in Choc Bits and nuts.

Beat 1 cup of the cream until firm peaks form, fold into white chocolate mixture. Beat egg whites until soft peaks form, fold into white chocolate mixture. Pour mixture evenly into 6 glasses (¾ cup capacity); refrigerate several hours or until set.

Combine dark chocolate and remaining cream in saucepan, stir constantly over low heat until mixture is smooth. Pour thin layer of warm dark chocolate over white chocolate mixture, swirl extra white chocolate through dark chocolate, refrigerate until set.

Serves 6.

MOCHA BAVARIAN WITH PECAN PRALINE

Dessert can be made up to a day ahead; keep, covered, in refrigerator. Recipe unsuitable to freeze.

1½ cups milk
1 tablespoon dry instant coffee
100g dark chocolate, chopped
4 egg yolks
¾ cup castor sugar
1 tablespoon gelatine
¼ cup water
300ml carton thickened cream
PECAN PRALINE
¼ cup sugar
1 tablespoon water
½ cup pecans, chopped
Combine milk, coffee and chocolate in small saucepan, stir over low heat,

without boiling, until chocolate is melted. Beat egg yolks and sugar in small bowl with electric mixer until thick and pale, gradually add hot milk mixture while motor is operating. Sprinkle gelatine over water, dissolve gelatine over hot water, stir into chocolate mixture.

Refrigerate until mixture is just beginning to set, stir occasionally. Fold in whipped cream and praline. Pour into 4 glasses, refrigerate several hours or until firm. Serve with extra whipped cream, if desired; sprinkle with reserved praline.

Pecan Praline: Combine sugar and water in small heavy-based saucepan, stir constantly over heat, without boiling, until sugar is dissolved. Bring to boil, boil rapidly, uncovered, without stirring, until syrup turns golden brown. Add nuts, pour onto greased oven tray, cool until set; chop roughly. Reserve 2 tablespoons praline for decoration (see glossary).

Serves 4.

WHITE CHOCOLATE AND HONEY MOUSSE

Mousse can be made a day ahead; keep, covered, in refrigerator. Recipe unsuitable to freeze.

4 eggs, separated
125g white chocolate, melted
2 tablespoons honey
300ml carton thickened cream
125g dark chocolate, chopped
50g white chocolate, melted, extra
Combine egg yolks, white chocolate and honey in saucepan, stir constantly over low heat, without boiling, until mixture thickens slightly; transfer to large bowl, cool to room temperature.

LEFT: Chunky Chocolate Pecan Flan.
ABOVE: Back: Mocha Bavarian with Pecan Praline; front: White Chocolate and Honey Mousse.

Placemat: Jeffcoat Stevenson (left). Parfait glasses: Decor Gifts; tiles: Northbridge Ceramic & Marble Centre (above)

CHOCOLATE PECAN PIE

Pie can be frozen for 2 months. Recipe unsuitable to microwave.

PASTRY
¾ cup plain flour
½ cup self-raising flour
2 tablespoons custard powder
90g butter
2 tablespoons water, approximately
CHOCOLATE PECAN FILLING
3 eggs, lightly beaten
1 cup light corn syrup
⅓ cup castor sugar
125g dark chocolate, melted
30g butter, melted
1½ cups (150g) pecans

Pastry: Combine sifted flours and custard powder in large bowl, rub in butter. Stir in enough water to make a firm dough. Knead dough on lightly floured surface until smooth, roll out large enough to line 23cm flan tin, trim edges; refrigerate 15 minutes.

Pour pecan mixture into pastry case. Bake in moderate oven for about 1 hour or until filling is set. Cool pie in flan tin.

Chocolate Pecan Filling: Combine eggs, corn syrup, sugar, chocolate and butter in bowl, stir in pecans.

ALMOND MERINGUE TORTE WITH CUSTARD CREAM

Tia Maria and Kahlua are coffee-flavoured liqueurs. Almond meringue layers can be made several days ahead of serving; keep in an airtight container. Torte is best served the day it is made. Recipe not suitable to freeze or microwave.

ALMOND MERINGUE
8 egg whites
1 cup castor sugar
1 cup packaged ground almonds
50g white chocolate, grated
CUSTARD CREAM
8 egg yolks
½ cup castor sugar
¾ cup cream
2 tablespoons Tia Maria or Kahlua
155g unsalted butter
3 teaspoons cocoa

Almond Meringue: Grease 2 x 20cm sandwich or deep cake pans, cover bases with paper, grease paper. Beat egg whites in large bowl until soft peaks form; gradually add sugar, beating well after each addition. Beat until sugar is dissolved; fold in almonds and chocolate.

Spread mixture into prepared pans,

bake in moderately slow oven for about 1¼ hours or until firm. Stand 5 minutes before turning onto wire rack, gently remove paper from bases; cool.

Place 1 layer of meringue onto serving plate, top with a layer of custard cream, cover with remaining meringue, spread all over with remaining custard cream, reserving some custard cream for decoration. Pipe decorations using reserved custard cream, top with chocolate curls (see glossary) and extra chocolate-dipped almonds, if desired.

Custard Cream: Combine egg yolks, sugar, cream and liqueur in saucepan, stir constantly over heat, without boiling, until sugar is dissolved and mixture has thickened slightly; cool to room temperature.

Cream butter in small bowl with electric mixer until light and fluffy, beat in sifted cocoa. Gradually add custard to butter mixture while motor is operating. Refrigerate 10 minutes before using.

ABOVE: Almond Meringue Torte with Custard Cream. RIGHT: Chocolate Pecan Pie.

China: Noritake (above)

CHOCOLATE CHERRY MERINGUE DESSERTS

Amaretto is an almond-flavoured liqueur. If you prefer a tart flavour, use the imported bottled morello cherries. Desserts can be layered in dishes several hours ahead; top with meringue just before serving. Plain chocolate cake can be bought from cake shops and some supermarkets. This recipe is unsuitable to freeze or microwave.

250g chocolate cake, chopped
½ cup sugar
½ cup water
¼ cup Amaretto
425g can cherries, drained
3 egg yolks
2 teaspoons cornflour
¼ cup sugar, extra
1½ cups milk
125g packet cream cheese, chopped
MERINGUE
3 egg whites
½ cup castor sugar

Divide cake into 6 ovenproof dishes (1 cup capacity). Combine sugar and water in saucepan, stir constantly over heat, without boiling, until sugar is dissolved; bring to boil, boil, uncovered, for 2 minutes, without stirring. Remove from heat, stir in liqueur, pour over cake in dishes. Divide cherries evenly into dishes.

Blend egg yolks, cornflour and extra sugar in saucepan, gradually stir in milk, stir constantly over heat until custard boils and thickens. Reduce heat, add cream cheese, stir over heat until melted; remove from heat. Divide custard evenly into dishes, stand 15 minutes. Spread evenly with the meringue, bake in moderately slow oven for about 12 minutes; increase oven temperature to moderate, bake further 5 minutes or until the meringue is lightly browned.

Meringue: Beat egg whites in small bowl with electric mixer until soft peaks form, gradually add sugar, beat until dissolved.

Serves 6.

CHOCOLATE MANDARIN ICE-CREAM RING

Prepare dessert a day before serving. You will need a 300ml carton cream and about 3 mandarins for this recipe. Dessert can be frozen for 2 months. Recipe unsuitable to microwave.

CHOCOLATE SPONGE
3 eggs
½ cup castor sugar
¼ cup self-raising flour
¼ cup cornflour
2 tablespoons plain flour
2 tablespoons cocoa
MANDARIN ICE-CREAM
1 teaspoon gelatine
¼ cup milk
½ cup castor sugar
½ cup water
2 teaspoons grated mandarin rind
⅓ cup mandarin juice
½ cup milk, extra

¾ **cup thickened cream**
orange colouring
CHOCOLATE SAUCE
125g dark chocolate, melted
½ **cup thickened cream**
Chocolate Sponge: Lightly grease and flour 23cm savarin tin or 20cm ring pan. Beat eggs in small bowl with electric mixer until thick and creamy. Gradually add sugar, beating until dissolved between each addition. Transfer mixture to large bowl, fold in sifted flours and cocoa.

Spoon mixture into prepared tin, bake in a moderate oven for about 30 minutes or until firm. Stand for 5 minutes before turning sponge onto wire rack to cool.

To form tunnel for ice-cream: Place strip plastic wrap to line savarin tin and extend well around edges. Return cake to lined tin. Carefully cut a circle from top of cake by cutting about 1cm from

inner and outer edges and about 2cm deep. Using teaspoon, scoop out centre, as pictured, leaving about 1cm shell of cake all around.

Fill centre with mandarin ice-cream and replace top of cake. Cover with plastic wrap, then foil; freeze overnight. Turn onto serving plate, serve topped with chocolate sauce.

Mandarin Ice-Cream: Sprinkle gelatine over milk, dissolve over hot water (or microwave on HIGH for about 15 seconds), combine sugar and water in saucepan, stir constantly over heat, without boiling, until sugar is dissolved. Remove from heat, add rind, juice and gelatine mixture, cool to room temperature. Add extra milk, cream and a little colouring, if desired.

Pour into lamington pan, cover with foil, freeze until nearly set. Place mixture into small bowl, beat with electric mixer until soft and smooth.
Chocolate Sauce: Stir chocolate and cream in small bowl until smooth.

LEFT: Chocolate Cherry Meringue Desserts. ABOVE: Chocolate Mandarin Ice-Cream Ring.

Fabric: Warwick Fabrics.

ALMOND CHOCOLATE BOMBE

Vienna almonds are toffee-coated almonds. Amaretto is an almond-flavoured liqueur. Dessert can be made up to 2 days ahead; keep, covered, in freezer. Stand 10 minutes at room temperature before serving.

100g dark chocolate, melted
100g milk chocolate, melted
100g white chocolate, melted
90g butter, melted
½ cup sultanas
2 tablespoons Amaretto
2 litre tub chocolate ice-cream
1 cup Vienna almonds, finely
**   chopped**

Line 6-cup capacity bowl with plastic wrap. Place each of the 3 types of chocolate in 3 small bowls; divide butter evenly between the bowls, stir each until smooth. Drop spoonfuls of each of the 3 mixtures over inside of lined bowl; lightly smooth surface with spatula, forming shell; freeze until set.

Combine sultanas and liqueur in saucepan, simmer 3 minutes or until most of the liqueur has been absorbed; cool. Soften ice-cream in large mixing bowl, stir in sultana mixture and almonds, pour into frozen chocolate shell. Freeze several hours or overnight. Turn onto serving plate, carefully peel away plastic wrap.

CHOCOLATE RASPBERRY TOWERS

Crème de Cacao is a chocolate-flavoured liqueur; Cointreau is an orange-flavoured liqueur. Towers are best assembled 2 hours ahead; keep in refrigerator. Chocolate biscuits can be frozen for up to 2 months. Recipe unsuitable to microwave.

CHOCOLATE BISCUITS
½ cup plain flour
½ cup self-raising flour
¼ cup icing sugar
60g dark chocolate, melted
1 egg, lightly beaten
200g punnet raspberries
1 tablespoon icing sugar, extra
1 tablespoon thickened cream
ORANGE CREAM
300ml carton thickened cream
2 teaspoons grated orange rind
2 teaspoons Cointreau
CHOCOLATE SAUCE
1 cup thickened cream
60g dark chocolate, melted
1 tablespoon Crème de Cacao

Chocolate Biscuits: Sift flours and icing sugar into bowl; stir in combined chocolate and egg in 2 batches; mix to a soft dough. Turn onto lightly floured surface, knead lightly until smooth, cover; refrigerate 15 minutes. Roll pastry between sheets of greaseproof paper to 3mm thick. Cut 12 x 9cm rounds from pastry, place about 2cm apart on lightly greased oven trays, bake in moderately hot oven for about 10 minutes or until firm; cool on trays.

Place 1 biscuit on each serving plate. Pipe or spread orange cream onto biscuits, top with 5 raspberries. Repeat layering with biscuits, orange cream and raspberries. Dust with extra sifted icing sugar. Serve with chocolate sauce.

To form hearts: Drop a tiny amount of cream into chocolate sauce, draw skewer through sauce and cream to create a heart shape; refrigerate.

Orange Cream: Beat cream in small bowl until firm peaks form; fold in rind and liqueur; refrigerate.

Chocolate Sauce: Combine cream, chocolate and liqueur in small bowl, stir until smooth; refrigerate until thick and pourable.

Serves 4.

FAR LEFT: Almond Chocolate Bombe.
BELOW: Chocolate Raspberry Towers.

Plate: Martinvale; tiles: Northbridge Ceramic & Marble Centre (far left). Plate: Mikasa (below)

FROZEN CHOCOLATE MOUSSE WITH STRAWBERRY SAUCE

Tia Maria and Kahlua are coffee-flavoured liqueurs.

30g butter, melted
185g dark chocolate, melted
3 eggs
¼ cup castor sugar
2 tablespoons Tia Maria or Kahlua
½ cup thickened cream
HAZELNUT PRALINE
¼ cup sugar
1 tablespoon water
⅓ cup roasted hazelnuts, chopped

STRAWBERRY SAUCE
250g fresh or frozen strawberries
1 tablespoon icing sugar,
**   approximately**
1 tablespoon thickened cream

Combine butter and chocolate in bowl, stir until smooth; cool to room temperature, do not allow to set.

Beat eggs and sugar in small bowl with electric mixer until thick and creamy; fold in chocolate mixture, liqueur and praline, then fold in whipped cream. Pour into 6 dishes (⅓ cup capacity), cover with foil. Freeze overnight or several hours until

set. Serve with strawberry sauce and extra whipped cream, if desired.

Hazelnut Praline: Combine sugar and water in saucepan, stir constantly over heat, without boiling, until sugar is dissolved; increase heat, boil, uncovered, without stirring, until golden brown. Add hazelnuts, pour onto greased tray. When set, chop praline finely. Any left-over praline can be stored in an airtight container for several months (see glossary).

Strawberry Sauce: Blend or process berries with enough icing sugar to sweeten to taste; strain, stir in cream.

80

WALNUT MACAROON PUDDINGS

Puddings are best prepared as close to serving time as possible. Recipe unsuitable to freeze or microwave.

1 cup walnuts
2 eggs, separated
1 tablespoon castor sugar
1 tablespoon brandy
¾ cup packaged macaroons, crushed
100g white chocolate, melted
2 tablespoons self-raising flour
30g unsalted butter, melted
2 tablespoons castor sugar, extra
CREAMY CHOCOLATE SAUCE
¾ cup thickened cream
100g milk chocolate, chopped

Lightly grease 4 heatproof moulds (1 cup capacity). Blend or process walnuts until finely ground. Beat egg yolks, sugar and brandy in small bowl with electric mixer until pale and thick. Transfer to large bowl, stir in nuts, macaroons and cooled chocolate, then sifted flour and butter.

Beat egg whites in small bowl with electric mixer until soft peaks form, gradually add extra sugar, beat until dissolved. Fold egg white mixture into nut mixture, divide mixture into prepared moulds.

Place into baking dish with enough hot water to come halfway up sides of moulds. Bake in moderately slow oven for about 1 hour or until puddings are set. Stand 5 minutes before turning onto serving plates. Serve with hot creamy chocolate sauce.

Creamy Chocolate Sauce: Combine cream and chocolate in small saucepan; stir constantly over heat, without boiling, until sauce is smooth and heated through.

Serves 4.

CHESTNUT CHOCOLATE BAVAROIS

Tia Maria and Kahlua are coffee-flavoured liqueurs; Kirsch is cherry-flavoured. Chestnut spread is an imported product available in gourmet sections of food stores; the spread contains sugar and flavouring. Recipe unsuitable to freeze or microwave.

4 egg yolks
¼ cup castor sugar
1 cup milk
90g dark chocolate, chopped
3 teaspoons gelatine
2 tablespoons water
250g can chestnut spread
300ml carton thickened cream
1 tablespoon Tia Maria or Kahlua
RASPBERRY SAUCE
250g fresh or frozen raspberries
½ cup icing sugar
1 tablespoon Kirsch

Beat egg yolks and sugar in small bowl with electric mixer until thick and creamy. Heat milk and chocolate in saucepan, stir constantly over heat, without boiling, until chocolate is melted. Stir into egg yolk mixture. Return to saucepan, stir constantly over low heat until mixture thickens slightly, do not boil; transfer to large bowl, cool about 5 minutes.

Sprinkle gelatine over water, dissolve over hot water (or microwave on HIGH for about 20 seconds), stir into chocolate mixture with chestnut spread; cool to room temperature. Beat cream and liqueur until soft peaks form, fold into chocolate mixture.

Divide mixture between 4 lightly oiled moulds (¾ cup capacity); refrigerate until set. Turn onto serving plates, serve with raspberry sauce.

Raspberry Sauce: Blend or process thawed raspberries, icing sugar and liqueur until smooth; sieve.

Serves 4.

ABOVE: Walnut Macaroon Puddings.
LEFT: Back: Frozen Chocolate Mousse with Strawberry Sauce; front: Chestnut Chocolate Bavarois.

Glassware: Dansab (left)

COFFEE TRUFFLE ICE-CREAM BOMBE

Tia Maria and Kahlua are coffee-flavoured liqueurs. Dessert can be made up to 3 days ahead.

1 tablespoon dry instant coffee
1 tablespoon hot water
3 eggs
½ cup castor sugar
2 x 300ml cartons thickened cream
2 tablespoons Tia Maria or Kahlua

CHOCOLATE TRUFFLES
100g dark chocolate, melted
60g butter, melted
2 tablespoons thickened cream
2 tablespoons icing sugar

CHOCOLATE SAUCE
100g dark chocolate, melted
½ cup thickened cream
1 tablespoon Tia Maria or Kahlua

Ice-Cream: Dissolve coffee in water in small bowl; cool. Whisk eggs and sugar in large saucepan over low heat until thick and frothy; do not boil; cool. Place cream, coffee mixture and liqueur in large bowl, beat with electric mixer until firm peaks form. Lightly fold egg mixture into cream; pour into slab pan, cover with foil, freeze until firm.

Place ice-cream into large bowl of electric mixer, beat until smooth. Spoon a layer of ice-cream into 1 litre (4 cup) mould, place some of the truffles over ice-cream. Repeat with remaining truffles and ice-cream. Cover with foil, freeze until set.

Chocolate Truffles: Combine chocolate and butter in small bowl, stir in cream and sifted icing sugar. Refrigerate until firm enough to roll into balls. Refrigerate truffles before use.

Chocolate Sauce: Combine chocolate, cream and liqueur in small bowl, stir until smooth.

ABOVE: Coffee Truffle Ice-Cream Bombe.

Plate: Lifestyle Imports (above)

CHOCOLATE ORANGE CHEESECAKE

Cointreau is a citrus-flavoured liqueur. Hazelnut spread, for example, Nutella, is available at supermarkets. Cheesecake can be made up to 2 days ahead; keep, covered, in refrigerator. Recipe unsuitable to freeze.

1 tablespoon gelatine
¼ cup water
1 cup plain sweet biscuit crumbs
90g butter, melted
250g packet cream cheese
⅓ cup icing sugar
2 x 300ml cartons thickened cream
150g dark chocolate, melted

2 tablespoons hazelnut spread
1 tablespoon Cointreau
2 teaspoons grated orange rind
orange colouring

Sprinkle gelatine over water, dissolve over hot water (or microwave on HIGH for about 20 seconds), cool to room temperature; do not allow to set. Combine crumbs and butter in bowl, mix well. Press firmly over base of 20cm springform tin; refrigerate while preparing filling.

Beat cream cheese in large bowl with electric mixer until smooth, beat in sifted icing sugar. Add cream, beat until just combined. Beat in gelatine mixture. Divide mixture into 2 bowls.

Add chocolate and hazelnut spread to 1 bowl. Add liqueur, rind and a little colouring to remaining bowl; mix well.

Refrigerate orange mixture about 5 minutes or until just beginning to set. Drop spoonfuls of both fillings over biscuit base, use knife to swirl mixture. Refrigerate several hours or overnight. Pipe cheesecake with extra whipped cream, if desired (see glossary) and decorate with extra chocolate.

BELOW: Chocolate Orange Cheesecake.

China: Dansab; fabric: Warwick Fabrics

RASPBERRY LACE BASKETS

Baskets can be made up to 3 days ahead; keep, covered, in refrigerator. Filling and sauce can be made up to a day ahead; keep, covered, in refrigerator. Baskets can be assembled several hours before serving. Recipe unsuitable to freeze or microwave.

300ml carton thickened cream
100g white chocolate, chopped
2 eggs, separated
2 tablespoons brandy
LACE BASKETS
200g White Melts, melted
50g dark chocolate, melted
BERRY ORANGE SAUCE
250g punnet raspberries

HOT CHOCOLATE SOUFFLES WITH CHERRY CREAM

Soufflés can be made several hours in advance up to the stage just before egg whites are folded through. Recipe unsuitable to freeze or microwave.

1 cup milk
125g dark chocolate, chopped
60g butter
1 tablespoon cornflour
2 tablespoons plain flour
⅓ cup castor sugar
4 eggs, separated
CHERRY CREAM
300ml carton thickened cream
1 tablespoon cherry brandy
red colouring
Grease 4 soufflé dishes (1 cup capacity), sprinkle with sugar.

Combine milk and chocolate in saucepan, stir constantly over heat, without boiling, until chocolate is melted. Melt butter in separate saucepan, add flours, cook, stirring, for 1 minute. Add chocolate mixture and sugar, stir constantly over heat until mixture boils and thickens.

Remove from heat, quickly stir in lightly beaten egg yolks. Beat egg whites in small bowl until soft peaks form, fold into chocolate mixture in 2 batches. Pour mixture into prepared dishes, bake in moderately hot oven for about 15 minutes. Serve immediately with cherry cream.

Cherry Cream: Combine cream and brandy in bowl, tint with a little colouring; beat until soft peaks form.

Serves 4.

2 tablespoons cranberry sauce
¼ cup orange juice
2 tablespoons icing sugar

Place ¼ cup of the cream in small saucepan, bring to boil, remove from heat, add white chocolate, stir until smooth. Transfer to large bowl, add egg yolks, beat with electric mixer until thick. Beat ½ cup of the remaining cream and brandy in small bowl until soft peaks form. Gently fold into egg yolk mixture.

Beat egg whites in bowl until soft peaks form, gently fold into egg yolk mixture, cover; refrigerate for about 2 hours or until set. Spoon into lace baskets. Beat remaining cream until firm, pipe around edge (see glossary),

decorate with raspberries. Serve with berry orange sauce.

Lace Baskets: Lightly oil inside 6 moulds (½ cup capacity), thinly coat with White Melts, refrigerate until coating is set.

Repeat twice more with chocolate. Remove baskets from moulds, pipe sides with dark chocolate, refrigerate until set.

Berry Orange Sauce: Blend or process ½ cup raspberries with remaining ingredients until smooth, sieve before serving. Reserve remaining raspberries for decoration.

Makes 6.

BELOW: Raspberry Lace Baskets.
LEFT: Hot Chocolate Soufflés with Cherry Cream.

Plate: Dansab (below)

PECAN CREPES WITH COFFEE SAUCE

Tia Maria and Kahlua are coffee-flavoured liqueurs. Filled crêpes can be prepared up to a day ahead; keep covered, in refrigerator. Make coffee sauce on day of serving. Recipe unsuitable to freeze or microwave.

CREPES
⅓ cup plain flour
2 eggs, lightly beaten
1 tablespoon oil
¾ cup milk
BUTTERY NUT FILLING
90g butter
½ cup pecans or walnuts, chopped
¼ cup icing sugar
COFFEE SAUCE
60g unsalted butter
125g white chocolate, chopped
¼ cup icing sugar
3 teaspoons dry instant coffee
1 teaspoon hot water
½ cup thickened cream
3 teaspoons Tia Maria or Kahlua
Crêpes: Sift flour into bowl, make well in centre. Gradually stir in eggs, oil and milk, beat until batter is smooth; cover, refrigerate 30 minutes.

Pour about ¼ cup batter into heated greased crêpe pan; cook until golden brown. Turn crêpe, cook other side. Repeat with remaining batter.

BAKED CHOCOLATE CUSTARD

Custard may develop a marbled effect during cooking. Recipe unsuitable to freeze or microwave.

3 eggs
¼ cup cocoa
⅓ cup castor sugar
2 cups milk
1 tablespoon icing sugar
Whisk eggs, sifted cocoa and sugar together in large bowl. Heat milk in a small saucepan, gradually whisk into egg mixture. Pour into 4 ovenproof dishes (¾ cup capacity).

Stand dishes in baking dish with enough hot water to come halfway up sides of dishes. Bake in moderate oven for 25 minutes, reduce heat to moderately slow, bake further 20 minutes or until set. Sprinkle with sifted icing sugar just before serving.
Serves 4.

ABOVE: Pecan Crêpes with Coffee Sauce. RIGHT: Baked Chocolate Custard. ABOVE RIGHT: Chocolate and Berry Meringue Flans.

China: Noritake; lace cloth: Village Living (above). Plate: Studio Kara; glass in background: Celtic Studios (far right)

Spread half of each crêpe evenly with filling, fold crêpes into triangles. Place crêpes, slightly overlapping, in lightly greased ovenproof dish. Cover, bake in moderate oven for about 15 minutes or until heated through. Serve with sauce and ice-cream, if desired.

Buttery Nut Filling: Combine softened butter, nuts and sifted icing sugar in a small bowl; mix well.

Coffee Sauce: Combine butter and chocolate in small saucepan, stir constantly over heat, without boiling, until smooth. Remove from heat, stir in sifted icing sugar, combined coffee and water, cream and liqueur. Return to heat, stir constantly, without boiling, until smooth.

CHOCOLATE AND BERRY MERINGUE FLANS

We used 10 fluted flan tins, 7cm in diameter, for this recipe. Any type of berry can be used. Recipe unsuitable to freeze or microwave.

PASTRY
¾ cup plain flour
¼ cup self-raising flour
1 tablespoon custard powder
90g butter, chopped
1 egg yolk
1 tablespoon lemon juice, approximately

BERRY LAYER
250g fresh or frozen berries
1 tablespoon icing sugar
1 tablespoon arrowroot
CHOCOLATE LAYER
2 egg yolks
2 tablespoons castor sugar
1 tablespoon plain flour
2 teaspoons cornflour
1 cup milk
75g dark chocolate, chopped
MERINGUE
3 egg whites
½ cup castor sugar

Pastry: Combine sifted flours and custard powder in large bowl, rub in butter. Add lightly beaten egg yolk and enough lemon juice to mix to a firm dough. Knead dough on lightly floured surface until smooth. Roll half the pastry between plastic wrap until pastry is large enough to line 5 flan tins. Repeat with remaining pastry.

Place flan tins onto oven tray, refrigerate 15 minutes. Bake in moderately hot oven for about 10 minutes or until lightly browned; cool in tins. Carefully remove flan cases from tins. Place cases on oven tray.

Place level tablespoonfuls of berry mixture into flan cases, refrigerate until berry mixture is set. Spoon chocolate mixture evenly over berry layer. Top with meringue, bake in moderately hot oven about 5 minutes or until browned.

Berry Layer: Blend or process berries and icing sugar until smooth; sieve. Blend small amount of berry mixture with arrowroot in saucepan, gradually stir in remaining berry mixture, stir constantly over heat (or microwave on HIGH for about 3 minutes), until mixture boils and thickens.

Chocolate Layer: Blend egg yolks, sugar and flours in saucepan until smooth, gradually stir in milk, stir constantly over heat until mixture boils and thickens. Remove from heat, add chocolate, stir until smooth.

Meringue: Beat egg whites in small bowl with electric mixer until soft peaks form, gradually add sugar, beat until dissolved between each addition.

Makes 10.

MACADAMIA GINGER TARTLETS

Tartlets can be made a day ahead; keep, covered, in refrigerator. Make sauce just before serving. Recipe unsuitable to freeze or microwave.

125g unsalted butter
2 tablespoons castor sugar
1 egg, lightly beaten
1½ cups plain flour
MACADAMIA GINGER FILLING
185g unsalted butter
⅓ cup castor sugar
¼ cup cream
2 tablespoons chopped glacé ginger
2 tablespoons mixed peel, chopped
⅓ cup pine nuts
¾ cup macadamia nuts, chopped
DARK AND WHITE COCONUT
    SAUCES
2 x 150g cans coconut milk
75g dark chocolate, chopped
75g white chocolate, chopped

Combine butter and sugar in small bowl, beat with electric mixer until combined; beat in egg, beat until just combined. Transfer mixture to large bowl, stir in sifted flour in 2 batches. Knead gently on lightly floured surface until smooth, cover, refrigerate 30 minutes. Roll pastry large enough to line 6 tartlet tins 9cm in diameter; trim.

Cover pastry with greaseproof paper, fill with dried beans or rice. Bake in moderate oven for 7 minutes, remove paper and beans, bake further 7 minutes or until golden brown.

Divide filling into pastry cases, bake in moderate oven for about 10 minutes or until golden brown. Serve with coconut sauces. Pour dark sauce into centre of each serving plate, top with tartlets, pour white sauce around tartlets. Using skewer, draw lines as pictured.

Macadamia Ginger Filling: Combine butter and sugar in small saucepan, stir constantly over heat, without boiling, until sugar is dissolved. Add remaining ingredients, bring to boil, remove from heat.

Dark and White Coconut Sauces: Combine half the coconut milk and all the dark chocolate in small saucepan, stir constantly over low heat without boiling, until smooth. Repeat separately with remaining coconut milk and white chocolate.

Makes 6.

PASSIONFRUIT CREAM OF HEARTS

You will need about 14 passionfruit for this recipe. Cream hearts and sauce can be prepared up to a day ahead; keep, covered, in refrigerator. Recipe unsuitable to freeze or microwave.

PASSIONFRUIT CREAM
3 egg yolks
½ cup castor sugar
¼ cup milk
¾ cup passionfruit pulp
2 teaspoons gelatine
¼ cup water
100g white chocolate, melted
300ml carton thickened cream
STRAWBERRY SAUCE
2 x 250g punnets strawberries
½ cup castor sugar
⅓ cup passionfruit pulp
Passionfruit Cream: Lightly oil 8 moulds (⅓ cup capacity). Combine egg yolks and sugar in small bowl, beat with electric mixer until thick and creamy. Heat milk in small saucepan, gradually add to egg mixture while motor is operating. Transfer to saucepan, stir constantly over heat, without boiling, until mixture thickens slightly. Remove from heat, add passionfruit.

Dissolve gelatine in water over hot water. Stir gelatine mixture and chocolate into passionfruit mixture; strain into large bowl. Refrigerate mixture until just starting to set.

Beat cream in small bowl until soft peaks form, fold into passionfruit mixture. Spoon into prepared moulds, refrigerate several hours or until set. Serve cream hearts with sauce.

Strawberry Sauce: Blend or process strawberries and sugar until smooth, stir in passionfruit; refrigerate.

Serves 8.

ABOVE: Passionfruit Cream of Hearts.
RIGHT: Macadamia Ginger Tartlets.

Plate: Casa Shopping (above)

BRANDY SNAP BASKETS WITH CURRANT LIQUEUR MOUSSE

Mousse can be made a day ahead. Baskets are best made on the day required as they soften on standing. Creme de Cassis is a black currant-flavoured liqueur. Recipe unsuitable to freeze or microwave.

3 tablespoons golden syrup
90g butter
⅓ cup brown sugar
½ cup plain flour
2 teaspoons ground ginger
CURRANT LIQUEUR MOUSSE
2 teaspoons gelatine
1 tablespoon water
150g White Melts, melted
4 eggs, separated
2 tablespoons Creme de Cassis
300ml carton thickened cream
pink colouring
RED CURRANT GLAZE
2 tablespoons red currant jelly
½ teaspoon arrowroot
1 tablespoon water
1 tablespoon Creme de Cassis

Combine golden syrup, butter and sugar in saucepan, stir constantly over heat, without boiling, until butter is melted. Remove from heat, stir in sifted flour and ginger.

Drop 2 heaped teaspoonfuls of mixture about 15cm apart onto lightly greased oven tray. For easy handling, bake only 2 brandy snaps at a time. Bake in moderate oven for about 5 minutes or until golden brown. Stand brandy snaps on tray for about 1 minute or until almost set, lift carefully from tray with spatula, below.

Immediately place brandy snaps over small moulds, above right. While brandy snaps are still pliable, mould with hands into basket shapes, cool on moulds. Continue to make baskets with remaining mixture. Fill baskets with mousse and drizzle with glaze just before serving.

RIGHT: Brandy Snap Baskets with Currant Liqueur Mousse. FAR RIGHT: Pears with Cointreau and Passionfruit Syrup.

Plate: Terrapotta (right)

Currant Liqueur Mousse: Sprinkle gelatine over water, dissolve over hot water (or microwave on HIGH for about 20 seconds). Combine dissolved gelatine, warm White Melts, lightly beaten egg yolks, liqueur and 2 tablespoons of the cream in small bowl, beat with electric mixer until combined; cool to room temperature.

Beat remaining cream in small bowl until soft peaks form. Beat egg whites in small bowl until soft peaks form. Gently fold cream, then egg whites, into liqueur mixture. Tint with pink colouring; refrigerate until set.

Red Currant Glaze: Combine jelly, blended arrowroot and water and liqueur in saucepan, stir constantly over heat until mixture comes up to the boil; cool to room temperature.

Makes 12.

PEARS WITH COINTREAU AND PASSIONFRUIT SYRUP

Cointreau is a citrus-flavoured liqueur. You will need about 10 passionfruit for this recipe. Pears can be prepared a day ahead. Cut stalk in half and leave attached to pears to achieve our finished effect, if desired. Recipe unsuitable to freeze or microwave.

3 ripe pears
1½ cups dry white wine
1 cup water
¾ cup castor sugar
3 teaspoons grated lemon rind
1 tablespoon lemon juice
5cm piece cinnamon stick

COINTREAU SAUCE
½ cup thickened cream
50g dark chocolate, chopped
1½ tablespoons Cointreau
PASSIONFRUIT SYRUP
½ cup passionfruit pulp
1 tablespoon sugar

Cut pears in half, remove cores. Combine wine, water, sugar, rind, juice and cinnamon in large saucepan, stir constantly over heat, without boiling, until sugar is dissolved. Bring syrup to boil, remove from heat, add pears in single layer, cover, cool to room temperature. Remove pears from wine syrup, reserve ¼ cup wine syrup for passionfruit syrup. Cut pears to form

fan shape, serve with sauce and passionfruit syrup.

Cointreau Sauce: Combine cream and chocolate in small saucepan, stir constantly over heat, without boiling, until smooth; remove from heat, stir in liqueur. Serve hot or cold.

Passionfruit Syrup: Combine passionfruit, reserved wine syrup and sugar in small saucepan, stir constantly over heat, without boiling, until sugar is dissolved. Bring to boil, reduce heat, simmer, uncovered, without stirring, for about 3 minutes or until sauce thickens slightly, strain to remove seeds; cool before serving.

Serves 6.

CHOCOLATE PECAN DREAM ICE-CREAM

Ice-cream can be made a week ahead; keep, covered, in freezer.

1½ x 300ml cartons thickened cream
100g dark chocolate, chopped
2 teaspoons dry instant coffee
4 egg yolks
½ cup castor sugar
1 tablespoon brandy
1 cup pecans or walnuts, chopped
100g dark chocolate, grated, extra

Combine cream, chocolate and coffee in medium saucepan, stir constantly over low heat, without boiling, until chocolate is melted; remove from heat. Beat egg yolks and sugar in small bowl with electric mixer until thick, gradually beat in hot cream mixture while motor is operating.

Return mixture to saucepan, stir over heat, without boiling, until mixture thickens slightly. Remove from heat, add brandy, pour into large bowl, cover. Cool to room temperature, pour into loaf pan, cover with foil, freeze several hours or until partly set. Remove from pan, beat in large bowl with electric mixer until smooth, stir in nuts and extra chocolate, return to pan, cover, freeze until set.

Makes about 1½ litres (6 cups).

CHOCOLATE STRAWBERRY MERINGUE DACQUOISE

Dessert is best made a day ahead for easier cutting. Recipe unsuitable to freeze or microwave.

4 egg whites
1 cup castor sugar
½ cup packaged ground almonds
2 tablespoons cocoa
300ml carton thickened cream
CHOCOLATE STRAWBERRY CREAM
¾ cup thickened cream
2 tablespoons icing sugar
100g dark chocolate, melted
250g punnet strawberries, chopped

Cover 2 oven trays with foil, grease and flour foil. Draw 20cm circle on each tray. Place egg whites in medium bowl, beat with electric mixer until soft peaks form. Gradually add sugar, beat until dissolved between each addition. Fold in almonds and sifted cocoa. Spoon mixture into piping bag fitted with large plain tube. Fill in circles, using drawn circles as a guide. Bake in slow oven for about 1 hour or until firm and dry; cool in oven with door ajar.

Peel away foil, sandwich meringues with chocolate strawberry cream. Top cake with lightly whipped cream, decorate with toasted flaked almonds and extra strawberries, if desired.
Chocolate Strawberry Cream: Whip cream and sifted icing sugar in small bowl until soft peaks form, stir in cooled chocolate and strawberries.

CHOCOLATE HAZELNUT STEAMED PUDDING

Tia Maria and Kahlua are coffee-flavoured liqueurs. Pudding is best prepared as close to serving time as possible. Recipe unsuitable to freeze or microwave.

4 eggs
1 cup castor sugar
125g unsalted butter, chopped
1 cup packaged ground
   hazelnuts
200g dark chocolate, coarsely grated
2 cups stale breadcrumbs
½ cup self-raising flour

COFFEE CREAM
300ml carton thickened cream
1 egg, lightly beaten
2 tablespoons Kahlua or Tia Maria
1 tablespoon castor sugar

Grease 6 cup capacity pudding mould. Beat eggs and sugar in small bowl with electric mixer until light and fluffy. Add butter gradually to egg mixture; beat until just combined. Transfer to large bowl. Fold in hazelnuts, chocolate, breadcrumbs and sifted flour.

Pour into prepared mould, cover with greased round of paper, then foil, secure with string or cover with lid. Place mould in large saucepan with enough boiling water to come halfway up side of mould; simmer, covered, for about 2½ hours or until firm. Serve hot with coffee cream.

Coffee Cream: Combine all ingredients in small saucepan, stir constantly over low heat, without boiling, until slightly thickened; strain before serving.

ABOVE: Chocolate Strawberry Meringue Dacquoise. LEFT: Chocolate Hazelnut Steamed Pudding. ABOVE LEFT: Chocolate Pecan Dream Ice-Cream.

China: Noritake (left). Plate, fork: Made Where (above)

ALMOND RUM DESSERT

Dessert is best prepared a day ahead; keep, covered, in refrigerator. Recipe unsuitable to freeze or microwave.

¼ cup castor sugar
2 tablespoons water
¼ cup packaged ground almonds
250g milk chocolate, melted
250g dark chocolate, melted
60g unsalted butter, melted
2 tablespoons white rum
1 tablespoon plain flour
2 teaspoons castor sugar, extra
2 eggs, separated
ALMOND CREAM
300ml carton thickened cream
⅓ cup icing sugar
¼ teaspoon almond essence

Grease 20cm springform tin, cover base with paper, grease paper. Combine sugar and water in small saucepan, stir constantly over heat, without boiling, until sugar is dissolved; bring to boil, boil, without stirring, until syrup turns golden brown. Add almonds, pour onto lightly greased oven tray; cool. When toffee is set, process until fine (see glossary).

Combine both chocolates, butter, rum, flour and extra sugar in large bowl, stir until smooth, stir in egg yolks. Beat egg whites in small bowl until soft peaks form, fold into chocolate mixture.

Spread into prepared tin, bake in moderately hot oven for 10 minutes; sprinkle cake with ¼ cup of the almond toffee mixture, bake further 10 minutes. Allow cake to cool in oven with door ajar. Refrigerate cake before serving with almond cream.

Almond Cream: Beat cream with sifted icing sugar in small bowl until soft peaks form, fold in remaining toffee and essence.

94

CHOCOLATE CREAM CONES

Kahlua and Tia Maria are coffee-flavoured liqueurs. Cones can be made and kept refrigerated for a week. Fill with cream just before serving. Recipe unsuitable to freeze.

200g dark chocolate, melted
300ml carton thickened cream
2 tablespoons icing sugar
1½ tablespoons Kahlua or Tia Maria

Cut 4 x 12cm circles from greaseproof or baking paper, shape each into a cone, make sure pointed end of each cone is completely closed, secure cones with tape.

Brush inside of each cone generously with a layer of chocolate; freeze until set.

Combine cream, sifted icing sugar and liqueur in small bowl, beat with electric mixer until soft peaks form. Pipe or spoon cream into each cone, refrigerate for 1 hour before serving. Serve with fresh fruit.

Makes 4.

LEFT: Chocolate Cream Cones.
FAR LEFT: Almond Rum Dessert.

Cake stand: Wedgwood; plate: Limoges; place mat: Studio-Haus; furniture: Kerry Trollope Antiques (far left)

ALMOND MINT SURPRISES

Crème de Menthe is a mint-flavoured liqueur. Cake can be prepared up to 2 days ahead. Only half the cake is used for this recipe; the other half can be frozen, undecorated, for up to 2 months for later use. Recipe unsuitable to microwave.

125g butter
⅓ cup castor sugar
3 eggs
¾ cup self-raising flour
¼ cup cocoa
¼ cup packaged ground almonds
32 square after-dinner mints
1 tablespoon apricot jam
1 tablespoon Crème de Menthe
MINT CREAM
300ml carton thickened cream
2 tablespoons icing sugar
1 tablespoon Crème de Menthe
green colouring

Grease deep 19cm square cake pan, cover base with paper, grease paper. Combine butter and sugar in small bowl, beat with electric mixer until light and fluffy. Add eggs 1 at a time, beat well between additions. Fold in sifted flour and cocoa and almonds.

Spread mixture into prepared pan, bake in moderate oven for about 25 minutes or until firm. Stand 5 minutes before turning onto wire rack to cool.

Cut cake in half vertically, trim ends from one half, cut into 8 x 4cm squares. Thinly spread smooth side of each mint with jam, press onto sides of each cake square to make a box. Sprinkle each square with a little of the liqueur.

Place mint cream into piping bag fitted with plain tube, pipe cream into each box, decorate as desired.

Mint Cream: Whip cream, sifted icing sugar and liqueur until firm peaks form; tint with colouring, if desired.

MILK CHOCOLATE RUM 'N' RAISIN MOUSSE

Mousse can be prepared up to 3 days ahead; keep, covered, in refrigerator. This recipe is unsuitable to freeze or microwave.

225g Milk Melts, melted
½ cup sour cream
3 eggs, separated
⅓ cup finely chopped raisins
1½ tablespoons dark rum
1 tablespoon toasted coconut
300ml carton thickened cream
2 tablespoons castor sugar

Combine Milk Melts, sour cream and egg yolks in large bowl, stir until smooth; add raisins, rum and coconut. Fold in lightly whipped cream. Beat egg whites in small bowl until soft peaks form, gradually beat in sugar, beat until dissolved, fold into chocolate mixture. Spoon into 6 serving glasses, decorate with flaked coconut and chocolate palm trees (see glossary).

Serves 6.

ABOVE: Almond Mint Surprises. RIGHT: Milk Chocolate Rum 'n' Raisin Mousse.

Glasses: Kosta Boda (right)

FROZEN MOCHA MOUSSE

Tia Maria and Kahlua are coffee-flavoured liqueurs. Hazelnut spread, for example, Nutella, is available from supermarkets. You will need about 2½ x 300ml cartons cream for this recipe. Mousse can be prepared up to a week ahead; keep, covered, in freezer.

DARK CHOCOLATE LAYER
100g dark chocolate, melted
2 teaspoons Tia Maria or Kahlua
2 eggs, separated
½ cup thickened cream
MILK CHOCOLATE LAYER
100g milk chocolate, melted
2 teaspoons Tia Maria or Kahlua
2 eggs, separated
½ cup thickened cream
WHITE CHOCOLATE LAYER
120g white chocolate, melted
60g butter, melted
2 teaspoons Tia Maria or Kahlua
3 eggs, separated
⅔ cup thickened cream
NUTTY CHOCOLATE SAUCE
½ cup hazelnut spread
¾ cup thickened cream
1 tablespoon Tia Maria or Kahlua

Dark Chocolate Layer: Line 14cm x 21cm loaf pan with plastic wrap. Combine chocolate, liqueur and egg yolks in large bowl, stir until smooth. Whip cream in small bowl until soft peaks form, fold into chocolate mixture. Beat egg whites in small bowl until soft peaks form, fold into chocolate mixture.

Pour chocolate mixture into prepared dish; cover with foil, freeze several hours or until firm. Top with milk chocolate layer, cover; freeze until firm. Top with white chocolate layer, cover; freeze until firm. Turn mousse onto serving plate; remove plastic wrap. Serve mousse sliced with nutty chocolate sauce.

Milk Chocolate Layer: Combine chocolate, liqueur and egg yolks in large bowl, stir until smooth. Fold in whipped cream and egg whites as for dark chocolate layer.

White Chocolate Layer: Combine chocolate, butter, liqueur and egg yolks in large bowl, stir until smooth. Fold in whipped cream and egg whites as for dark chocolate layer.

Nutty Chocolate Sauce: Place hazelnut spread in heatproof bowl, stir over hot water until pourable (or microwave on HIGH for about 30 seconds), gradually stir in cream and liqueur, refrigerate until cool.

LEFT: Frozen Mocha Mousse.
RIGHT: Chocolate Pear Puff.

Plate: Reflections Gift Boutique (left)

CHOCOLATE PEAR PUFF

Puff is best prepared as close to serving time as possible. Recipe unsuitable to freeze or microwave.

2 sheets ready-rolled puff pastry
425g can pear halves, drained, chopped
1 egg yolk
1 tablespoon milk
2 teaspoons icing sugar
CAKE
60g butter
¼ cup castor sugar
1 egg
⅓ cup sour cream
½ cup self-raising flour
1 tablespoon cocoa
¼ cup packaged ground almonds

Cut 20cm round and 23cm round from pastry sheets.

Place small round of pastry onto lightly greased oven tray, spread cake mixture evenly over pastry, leaving 1cm border; top with pears. Brush border of pastry with combined egg yolk and milk. Place large round of pastry on top of pears, press edges together; mark top and side with knife to decorate. Brush evenly all over with egg yolk mixture.

Bake in moderately hot oven for 10 minutes, reduce to moderate, bake further 25 minutes or until golden brown. Dust with sifted icing sugar, place under hot grill, grill until sugar is melted and lightly browned.

Cake: Beat butter and sugar in small bowl with electric mixer until light and fluffy; add egg, beat until combined. Stir in sour cream and sifted flour and cocoa, then almonds.

MOCHA CHEQUERBOARD MOUSSE

Kahlua and Tia Maria are coffee-flavoured liqueurs. Mousse can be prepared up to 2 days ahead; keep, covered, in refrigerator. Recipe unsuitable to freeze.

CHOCOLATE MOUSSE
200g dark chocolate, melted
100g unsalted butter, melted
2 tablespoons Kahlua or Tia Maria
4 eggs, lightly beaten
1 tablespoon gelatine
⅓ cup water
300ml carton thickened cream
COFFEE MOUSSE
200g white chocolate, melted
100g unsalted butter, melted
2 tablespoons Kahlua or Tia Maria
4 eggs, lightly beaten
1 tablespoon dry instant coffee
½ cup water
1 tablespoon gelatine
1 cup thickened cream

Chocolate Mousse: Lightly oil 14cm x 21cm loaf pan. Combine chocolate, butter, liqueur and eggs in large bowl; stir until smooth. Sprinkle gelatine over water, dissolve over hot water (or microwave on HIGH for about 30 seconds); stir cooled gelatine into chocolate mixture. Beat cream until soft peaks form, fold into chocolate mixture. Refrigerate mousse until almost set; stir occasionally.

Fit large piping bag with large plain tube; fill with chocolate mousse. Fit another large piping bag with large plain tube; fill with coffee mousse. Pipe alternate rows of mousse into prepared pan; smooth each layer with spatula as it is completed. Cover, refrigerate until set. Turn mousse from pan, serve mousse sliced with fresh fruit, if desired.

Coffee Mousse: Combine chocolate, butter, liqueur and eggs in large bowl; stir until smooth. Dissolve coffee in water, sprinkle gelatine over coffee, dissolve over hot water (or microwave on HIGH for about 30 seconds). Stir gelatine mixture into chocolate mixture. Beat cream until soft peaks form, fold into chocolate mixture. Refrigerate mousse until almost set; stir occasionally.

TROPICAL RICE RING

Rice ring and sauce can be prepared up to 4 days ahead; keep, covered, in refrigerator. Recipe unsuitable to freeze or microwave.

2⅓ cups milk
½ cup water
½ cup sugar
¾ cup short grain rice
200g White Melts
2 teaspoons gelatine
1 tablespoon water, extra
¼ cup chopped glacé apricots
¼ cup chopped glacé pineapple
¼ cup sultanas
300ml carton thickened cream
APRICOT SAUCE
1 cup apricot nectar
2 teaspoons sugar
¼ cup chopped dried apricots
2 teaspoons cornflour
1 tablespoon water

Lightly oil 20cm baba or ring pan (6 cup capacity), sprinkle evenly with a little castor sugar. Combine milk, water and sugar in medium saucepan, stir constantly over heat, without boiling, until sugar is dissolved. Bring to boil, add rice, stir constantly over heat until mixture returns to boil.

Reduce heat, cover, cook over low heat for about 30 minutes or until nearly all the milk is absorbed. Remove from heat, add White Melts, stir until melted; cool to room temperature.

Sprinkle gelatine over extra water, dissolve over hot water, stir into rice mixture with fruit. Fold in lightly whipped cream. Spoon mixture into prepared mould, cover, refrigerate until firm. Turn onto serving plate, serve with apricot sauce.

Apricot Sauce: Combine nectar, sugar and apricots in small saucepan, bring to boil. Blend cornflour with water, stir into apricot mixture, stir constantly over heat until mixture boils and thickens, cool.

ABOVE: Mocha Chequerboard Mousse.
RIGHT: Tropical Rice Ring.

Tiles: Pazotti (above). Plate & scarf: Studio Kara (right)

Confections Plus

We're nuts about chocolate, and there are lashings of both (and lots more) in our rich, rich, rich little treats that are perfect with after-dinner coffee or afternoon tea. Every bite will delight you and your guests.

LEFT: Chocolate Nougat. FAR LEFT: Toffee Almond Cherries.

Plate: Made Where; table: Cebu Cane; fabric: Les Olivades (left). China and napkin: Studio-Haus; background: Cebu Cane (far left)

TOFFEE ALMOND CHERRIES

Prepare cherries as close to serving time as possible. You will need to buy a 200g roll prepared marzipan; keep remainder, covered, in refrigerator. Recipe unsuitable to freeze or microwave.

20 seedless maraschino cherries, with stems
20g prepared marzipan
CHOCOLATE TOFFEE
1 cup castor sugar
½ cup water
60g Choc Melts, finely chopped

Wash cherries and dry thoroughly. Make small cut in base of each cherry and fill with small piece of marzipan, press to enclose. Thinly coat each cherry with chocolate toffee. Place on greased oven tray, leave at room temperature to set.

Chocolate Toffee: Combine sugar and water in medium heavy-based saucepan, stir constantly over heat, without boiling, until sugar is dissolved. Bring to boil, boil rapidly, without stirring, for about 10 minutes or until golden brown. Remove from heat.

Place chocolate in heatproof bowl, slowly stir in toffee mixture a little at a time, mix quickly until all the toffee is incorporated. Do not over-mix, as toffee may crystallise. If toffee starts to set, stir gently over low heat until toffee liquefies.

Makes 20.

CHOCOLATE NOUGAT

For perfect results you should use a candy thermometer for this recipe. Rice paper is edible and can be bought from Asian stores and gourmet food shops. Nougat can be prepared up to a week ahead; keep, covered, in refrigerator. Recipe unsuitable to freeze or microwave.

2 sheets rice paper
1 cup castor sugar
1 tablespoon glucose syrup
⅓ cup water
¼ cup honey
1 egg white
¼ cup icing sugar
½ cup toasted almonds, chopped
½ cup Choc Bits

Cover base of deep 15cm square cake pan with sheet of rice paper. Combine sugar, glucose and water in medium heavy-based saucepan, stir constantly over heat, without boiling, until sugar is

dissolved. Bring to boil, boil rapidly, uncovered, without stirring, until syrup reaches "small crack" (or 138 degrees C or 280 degrees F). Heat honey in small heavy-based saucepan until it reaches "hard ball" (or 121 degrees C or 250 degrees F).

Place egg white in small bowl, beat on high speed with electric mixer until stiff. Gradually pour in hot sugar syrup in a thin steady stream while motor is operating. Beat in hot honey, then sifted icing sugar; quickly stir in nuts and Choc Bits.

Spread quickly into prepared pan, top with remaining piece of rice paper, press firmly onto nougat. Allow to set at room temperature before removing from pan and cutting.

COCONUT PISTACHIO TRUFFLES

Malibu is a coconut-flavoured liqueur. Truffles will keep, covered, in refrigerator for a month. Recipe unsuitable to freeze.

375g white chocolate, melted
¼ cup evaporated milk, warmed
1 tablespoon Malibu
½ teaspoon grated lemon rind
½ cup coconut
¼ cup pistachio nuts, chopped

Combine white chocolate and milk in bowl, stir until smooth; stir in liqueur and rind; refrigerate until set. Combine coconut and nuts in small frying pan, stir constantly over heat until coconut is lightly browned; cool.

Roll rounded teaspoonfuls of white chocolate mixture into balls, toss in coconut mixture, refrigerate balls before serving.

Makes about 35.

PEANUT SOFT CENTRES

Sweets can be made up to 2 weeks ahead; keep, covered, in refrigerator. Recipe unsuitable to freeze.

½ cup crunchy unsalted peanut butter
2 tablespoons icing sugar
1½ tablespoons cocoa

100g dark chocolate, melted
30g milk chocolate, melted

Combine peanut butter, sifted icing sugar and cocoa in small bowl, mix well, cover; refrigerate until firm. Roll mixture into 25cm roll, cut into 24 pieces, place on foil-covered tray, freeze 2 hours. Dip each piece in dark chocolate, return to tray to set at room temperature. Drizzle or pipe with milk chocolate.

Makes 24.

ABOVE: Coconut Pistachio Truffles.
RIGHT: Peanut Soft Centres. ABOVE RIGHT: Chocolate Fruit and Nut Bread.

Plate: Studio-Haus; background: Made Where (above). China: Mikasa; table: Cebu Cane (above right). China: Wedgwood (right)

CHOCOLATE FRUIT AND NUT BREAD

Bread will keep for up to 2 weeks in an airtight container. Recipe unsuitable to freeze or microwave.

3 egg whites
½ cup castor sugar
1 cup plain flour
¾ cup unroasted hazelnuts
⅓ cup chopped glacé apricots
¼ cup Choc Bits

Grease 7cm x 25cm bar pan. Beat egg whites in small bowl with electric mixer until soft peaks form, gradually add sugar, beat until dissolved after each addition. Fold in sifted flour, hazelnuts, apricots and Choc Bits.

Spread mixture into prepared pan, bake in moderate oven for about 30 minutes or until firm; cool in pan. Remove bread from pan, wrap in foil; stand in a cool place for 1 to 2 days.

Cut bread into wafer thin slices, place in single layer on oven trays. Bake in very slow oven for about 35 minutes or until dry and crisp. Stand on trays for 10 minutes, carefully remove from trays to wire rack to cool.

constantly over heat, without boiling, until sugar is dissolved; bring to boil, boil, uncovered, without stirring, until golden brown. Add nuts, pour onto greased oven tray, spread mixture as thinly as possible. When set, crush nut toffee into small pieces. Combine toffee and chocolate in small bowl. Drop rounded teaspoonfuls of mixture onto lightly greased tray, refrigerate until set.

Makes about 24.

CHOCOLATE MARSHMALLOW NUT FUDGE

Fudge can be made up to a week ahead; keep, covered, in refrigerator. This recipe is unsuitable to freeze or microwave.

2 x 100g packets white marshmallows
60g unsalted butter
1 tablespoon cream
125g dark chocolate, chopped
1 teaspoon vanilla essence
1 cup macadamia nuts, chopped
Grease 8cm x 26cm bar pan, line base and sides with foil, grease foil. Combine marshmallows, butter and cream in saucepan. Stir constantly over low heat until marshmallows are melted. Remove from heat, add chocolate and essence, stir until chocolate is melted. Beat for 1 minute with wooden spoon, add nuts, beat 30 seconds or until mixture is combined. Pour into prepared pan; refrigerate until set before cutting.

RICH DARK CHOCOLATE MINT FUDGE

Fudge can be made up to a month ahead; keep, covered, in refrigerator. Recipe unsuitable to freeze.

500g Choc Bits
400g can sweetened condensed milk
60g butter
peppermint essence
100g Milk Melts, melted
Into 19cm x 29cm lamington pan place strip of foil to cover base and extend over 2 opposite ends. Combine Choc Bits, condensed milk and butter in large saucepan, stir constantly over low heat, without boiling, until smooth (or microwave on HIGH for about 3 minutes). Add essence to taste, mix well. Spread evenly into prepared pan, cover, refrigerate until set before cutting. Drizzle or pipe with Milk Melts, refrigerate until set.

CHOCOLATE MARBLE ROUGHS

Roughs can be made up to a week ahead; keep, covered, in refrigerator. This recipe is unsuitable to freeze or microwave.

1 cup coconut, toasted
90g Milk Melts, melted
90g White Melts, melted
chopped glacé cherries
Combine half the coconut in small bowl with Milk Melts. Combine remaining coconut with White Melts in medium bowl. Gently mix coconut mixtures together for a marbled effect. Drop rounded teaspoonfuls of mixture onto tray covered with greaseproof paper, top with pieces of cherry, refrigerate until set.

Makes about 24.

NUTTY CHOCOLATE CLUSTERS

Clusters can be prepared up to a week ahead; keep, covered, in airtight container. Recipe unsuitable to freeze or microwave.

½ cup castor sugar
⅓ cup water
¼ cup finely chopped mixed nuts
125g milk chocolate, melted
Place sugar and water in saucepan, stir

CHERRY MARSHMALLOW SLICE

Slice will keep, covered, in refrigerator for a month. This recipe is unsuitable to freeze.

**2 x 100g packets white
     marshmallows, chopped
250g dark chocolate, chopped
125g unsalted butter, chopped
1 tablespoon water
½ cup glacé cherries, chopped**

Grease 7cm x 25cm bar pan, line base and sides with foil. Reserve ⅔ cup marshmallows. Combine remaining marshmallows with chocolate, butter and water in saucepan, stir constantly over low heat until mixture is smooth (or microwave on HIGH for about 3 minutes). Remove from heat, stand 10 minutes, stir in reserved marshmallows and cherries. Pour mixture into prepared pan, cover, refrigerate several hours or until set. Remove slice from pan before cutting.

COLETTES

Cointreau is a citrus-flavoured liqueur. Colettes will keep, covered, in refrigerator for up to 2 weeks. Recipe unsuitable to freeze or microwave.

**150g White Melts, melted
100g dark chocolate, melted
15g unsalted butter, melted
⅓ cup thickened cream
1 tablespoon Cointreau**

Using a small paint brush, paint White Melts over base and sides of foil confectionery cases; refrigerate until set.

Peel foil cases from chocolate. Combine dark chocolate and butter in bowl, gradually stir in cream and liqueur. Refrigerate chocolate mixture until thick enough to pipe. Fit piping bag with small fluted tube; fill with chocolate mixture. Pipe mixture into cases; refrigerate before serving.

Makes about 24.

HAZELNUT APRICOT TRUFFLES

Truffles will keep, covered, in refrigerator for several weeks. Recipe unsuitable to freeze or microwave.

**1 cup castor sugar
1 cup water
3 cups (300g) packaged ground
     hazelnuts
1 cup chopped glacé apricots
¼ cup cocoa
2 teaspoons lemon juice
1 cup icing sugar
400g dark chocolate, melted
½ cup chopped glacé apricots, extra
300g dark chocolate, melted, extra**

Combine sugar and water in medium saucepan, stir constantly over heat, without boiling, until sugar is dissolved. Bring to boil, boil 5 minutes, uncovered, without stirring; remove from heat.

Add nuts, apricots, cocoa and juice to sugar syrup, cook over low heat, without stirring, for about 2 minutes or until slightly thickened. Stir in sifted icing sugar and chocolate in 2 batches.

Spread mixture onto tray to cool to room temperature. Roll level teaspoonfuls of mixture into balls around a piece of extra glacé apricot. Place on tray, refrigerate several hours or overnight. Dip truffles in extra chocolate; place on foil-covered tray; refrigerate until set.

Makes about 45.

BELOW: From left: Colettes; Cherry Liqueur Cups; Chocolate Rum Truffles; Hazelnut Apricot Truffles. LEFT: Cherry Marshmallow Slice.

Plate: Strange Cargo Antiques (left); glass platter: Dansab (below)

CHERRY LIQUEUR CUPS

Cups can be prepared up to a week ahead; keep, covered, in refrigerator. Recipe unsuitable to freeze.

12 glacé cherries, halved
¼ cup cherry brandy
200g dark chocolate, melted
Combine cherries and brandy in small bowl, cover, stand overnight.

Remove cherries from brandy; reserve brandy. Combine reserved brandy and chocolate in small bowl, stir until smooth. Spoon small amount of chocolate into foil confectionery cases. Place half a cherry in each case, top with enough chocolate to fill cases, top with extra cherry, if desired.

Makes 24.

CHOCOLATE RUM TRUFFLES

Truffles can be made 3 days ahead; keep, covered, in refrigerator. Recipe unsuitable to freeze.

100g dark chocolate, melted
1½ tablespoons dark rum
2 tablespoons cream
30g butter, melted
1¾ cups icing sugar
1 cup packaged ground almonds
¼ cup cocoa
Combine chocolate, rum, cream and butter in bowl. Stir in sifted icing sugar and almonds in 2 batches. Cover, refrigerate until firm. Shape rounded teaspoonfuls of mixture into balls, roll in cocoa, place in small confectionery cases, refrigerate before serving.

Makes about 15.

CHOCOLATE CREAM PECAN TARTLETS

Pastry cases can be made a day ahead or frozen for up to 2 months. Chocolate cream filling can be prepared up to a day ahead; keep, covered, in refrigerator and bring to room temperature before using. Tartlets can be assembled up to 3 hours ahead. Recipe unsuitable to microwave.

PASTRY
1 cup plain flour
2 tablespoons icing sugar
60g unsalted butter
1 egg yolk
1 tablespoon water, approximately
30 pecan halves (about ⅔ cup)
CHOCOLATE CREAM FILLING
300g dark chocolate, melted
¾ cup thickened cream
Pastry: Sift flour and icing sugar into bowl, rub in butter. Add egg yolk and enough water to mix to a firm dough. Turn onto lightly floured surface, knead lightly until smooth, cover; refrigerate 30 minutes.

Roll pastry out to 3mm thick. Cut 5cm rounds from pastry, line small tartlet tins. Prick pastry all over with fork, bake in moderately hot oven for about 10 minutes or until lightly browned; cool.

Spoon filling into piping bag fitted with small fluted tube. Pipe filling into pastry cases, top with nuts; pipe remaining filling around nuts.

Chocolate Cream Filling: Combine chocolate and cream in small bowl; stir until smooth. Refrigerate, stirring occasionally, until mixture becomes a piping consistency.

Makes about 30.

MARZIPAN CHOCOLATES

Chocolates can be prepared up to a week ahead; keep, covered, in refrigerator. This recipe is unsuitable to freeze.

200g roll prepared marzipan
150g dark chocolate, melted
whole blanched almonds
50g Milk Melts, melted
Gently roll marzipan to sausage-shape about 20cm long, trim ends, cut into 1cm slices. Dip slices into dark chocolate, place slices onto foil-covered tray, top with almonds, allow to set at room temperature. Drizzle each chocolate with Milk Melts.

Makes about 18.

ABOVE: Marzipan Chocolates. RIGHT: From outside: Chocolate Cream Pecan Tartlets; Chocolate Palmiers.

China: Wedgwood; tray: Strange Cargo Antiques (above)

CHOCOLATE PALMIERS

Palmiers can be prepared several hours ahead. Recipe unsuitable to freeze or microwave.

375g packet frozen puff pastry, thawed
1 egg, lightly beaten
1 tablespoon castor sugar
¼ teaspoon ground cinnamon
200g dark chocolate, melted
Cut pastry into quarters. Roll out each quarter of pastry to a rectangle measuring 14cm x 19cm. Brush pastry lightly with egg, sprinkle evenly with about quarter of the combined sugar and cinnamon.

Fold long edges of pastry in so they meet edge to edge in centre, brush lightly with egg.

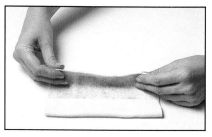

Bring folds over again so there are 4 even layers of pastry.

Using a sharp knife, cut pastry crossways into 1cm pieces.

Place about 2cm apart on lightly greased oven trays, spread them open at folded ends to make a small v.

Refrigerate 15 minutes.

Bake in hot oven for 5 minutes, turn palmiers over, bake further 5 minutes or until crisp and lightly browned; cool on wire racks. Repeat with remaining pastry. Dip 1 side of each palmier into chocolate. Place on foil-covered trays; allow to set at room temperature.

Makes about 60.

PEANUT SQUARES

Squares can be made 3 days ahead; keep, covered, in refrigerator. Recipe unsuitable to freeze or microwave.

125g unsalted butter
2 tablespoons milk
200g dark chocolate, chopped
3¼ cups icing sugar
½ cup unsalted roasted peanuts, chopped

Into 19cm x 29cm lamington pan place strip of foil to cover base and extend over 2 opposite ends.

Combine all ingredients in large heavy-based saucepan. Stir constantly and vigorously over medium heat, without boiling, for about 10 minutes or until mixture just begins to coat base of saucepan.

Spread into prepared pan, cool, cover, refrigerate for about 1 hour or until set before cutting.

ABOVE: Peanut Squares. RIGHT: Clockwise from top: Chocolate Nuts; Hazelnut Clusters; Chocolate Ginger and Almond Dates.

112

CHOCOLATE GINGER AND ALMOND DATES

Amaretto is an almond-flavoured liqueur. Dates can be prepared a day ahead, keep, covered, in refrigerator. Recipe unsuitable to freeze.

375g fresh dates
30g unsalted butter
1 cup flaked almonds
2 tablespoons castor sugar
2 teaspoons Amaretto
1 egg yolk
1 tablespoon chopped glacé ginger
200g dark chocolate, melted
60g unsalted butter, melted, extra
Carefully remove stones from dates. Melt butter in saucepan, add almonds, stir constantly over heat until almonds are lightly browned. Process almonds, sugar, liqueur, egg yolk and ginger until smooth. Fill dates with almond mixture, refrigerate 15 minutes.

Combine chocolate and extra butter in small bowl, dip dates into chocolate mixture, drain off excess chocolate. Place dates onto foil-covered tray, refrigerate for about 30 minutes or until set. Slice dates before serving.

HAZELNUT CLUSTERS

Clusters can be made 3 days ahead; keep, covered, in refrigerator. Recipe unsuitable to freeze.

100g dark chocolate, melted
¾ cup roasted hazelnuts
50g white chocolate, melted
15g butter, melted
Combine dark chocolate and hazelnuts in bowl, mix well. Drop level teaspoonfuls of mixture onto foil-covered tray; allow to set at room temperature. Combine white chocolate and butter in small bowl, stir until smooth. Drizzle or pipe chocolate mixture over each cluster.

Makes about 25.

CHOCOLATE NUTS

Chocolates can be prepared 3 days ahead; keep, covered, in refrigerator. Recipe unsuitable to freeze.

200g dark chocolate, melted
¼ cup almonds
50g dark chocolate melted, extra
15g butter, melted
Drop rounded teaspoonfuls of chocolate onto foil-covered tray, top each with an almond; allow to set at room temperature. Combine extra chocolate and butter in bowl, stir until smooth; drizzle or pipe mixture over each chocolate.

Makes about 15.

Background: Strange Cargo Antiques (far left).
China: Mikasa; background: Cebu Cane (left)

JEWEL DELIGHTS

Buy a good-quality Turkish Delight. Sweets can be made a week ahead; keep, covered, in refrigerator.

100g Turkish Delight
200g white chocolate, melted
60g butter, melted
¼ cup pistachio nuts
¾ cup Brazil nuts, coarsely chopped
¼ cup flaked coconut
200g milk chocolate, melted
60g butter, melted, extra
¼ cup toasted coconut

Chop Turkish Delight into ½cm cubes. Combine white chocolate and butter in medium bowl, stir until smooth; stir in nuts, coconut and Turkish Delight. Spoon mixture onto sheet of greaseproof or baking paper or foil, roll into a sausage shape about 4cm in diameter. Roll mixture up in the paper, refrigerate 1 hour.

Combine milk chocolate and extra butter in small bowl, stir until smooth; brush all over roll. Sprinkle all over with toasted coconut, refrigerate until firm. Stand roll at room temperature before slicing. Refrigerate before serving.

PINEAPPLE GINGER BITES

Grand Marnier is an orange-flavoured liqueur. Sweets can be made up to 2 weeks ahead; keep, covered, in refrigerator. This recipe is unsuitable to freeze.

3 rings glacé pineapple, finely chopped
2 tablespoons finely chopped glacé ginger
2 tablespoons Grand Marnier
½ cup thickened cream
250g milk chocolate, chopped
1 cup macadamia nuts, finely chopped

Combine pineapple, ginger and liqueur in small bowl, cover, stand for a few hours or overnight.

Place cream in small saucepan, bring to boil, remove from heat, add chocolate to cream, stir until smooth; stir in liqueur mixture. Cover, refrigerate until firm enough to handle. Roll rounded teaspoonfuls of mixture into balls, roll in nuts. Refrigerate on trays before serving.

Makes about 40.

BOUNTIFUL COCONUT BARS

Bars can be made up to a week ahead; keep, covered, in refrigerator. Recipe unsuitable to freeze or microwave.

½ cup castor sugar
¼ cup milk
1⅔ cups coconut
1 egg white, lightly beaten
¼ cup icing sugar
1 ring glacé pineapple
CHOCOLATE TOPPING
100g Milk Melts, melted
3 teaspoons oil

Combine sugar and milk in small saucepan, stir constantly over heat, without boiling, until sugar is dissolved, remove from heat; cool 5 minutes. Transfer to large bowl. Stir in coconut, egg white and sifted icing sugar. Place mixture into piping bag fitted with plain tube. Pipe bars onto greaseproof paper-covered tray, top with thin pieces of pineapple while moist, refrigerate until firm. Carefully cut into 2cm lengths, reshape into bars. Pour topping evenly over bars, move bars to coat bases, allow to set at room temperature.

Chocolate Topping: Combine hot chocolate and oil in small bowl; stir until smooth and pourable.

Makes about 60.

PECAN MALLOW ROUNDS

Rounds can be made up to 3 days ahead; keep, covered, in refrigerator. Recipe unsuitable to freeze.

⅓ cup thickened cream
250g Choc Bits
1 cup pecans or walnuts, finely chopped
100g packet white marshmallows, chopped
¼ cup coconut
2 teaspoons vanilla essence
100g Milk Bits, melted
3 teaspoons oil

Into 19cm x 29cm lamington pan place strip of foil to cover base and extend over 2 opposite ends.

Place cream in small saucepan, bring to boil (or microwave on HIGH for about 3 minutes). Remove from heat, add Choc Bits, stir until smooth, transfer to large bowl, stir in nuts, marshmallows, coconut and essence.

Press mixture evenly into prepared pan, cover, refrigerate for about 30 minutes or until set. Roll rounded teaspoonfuls of mixture into balls, dip into combined Milk Bits and oil, place onto wire rack over tray, set at room temperature. Drizzle or pipe with remaining Milk Bits mixture.

Makes about 40.

HONEY SNAP CONES WITH CHOCOLATE CREAM

Grand Marnier is an orange-flavoured liqueur. Cones are best made as close to serving time as possible. Fill with chocolate cream just before serving. This recipe is unsuitable to freeze or microwave.

30g butter
30g dark chocolate, chopped
2 tablespoons brown sugar
1½ tablespoons honey
¼ cup plain flour
CHOCOLATE CREAM
¾ cup thickened cream
1 tablespoon Grand Marnier
1 tablespoon icing sugar
50g dark chocolate, melted

Combine butter, chocolate, sugar and honey in saucepan, stir constantly over low heat until mixture is smooth. Remove from heat, stir in sifted flour.

Drop level teaspoonfuls of mixture onto lightly greased oven trays. For easy handling, bake only 2 honey snaps at a time. Bake in moderate oven for about 5 minutes or until just beginning to set around edges. Cool on tray for about 1 minute or until almost set; lift from tray with spatula.

Immediately wrap honey snaps around small cream horn tins, leave on tins until cool and crisp. Carefully remove from tins. Continue to make cones with remaining mixture. Pipe chocolate cream into each cone.

Chocolate Cream: Beat cream, liqueur and sifted icing sugar until soft peaks form, quickly stir in cooled chocolate.
Makes about 15.

CHOCOLATE THINS

Thins can be made up to 2 days ahead; keep, covered, in refrigerator. Recipe unsuitable to freeze.

100g dark chocolate, melted
30g unsalted butter, melted
1 cup icing sugar
2 teaspoons oil
1 tablespoon milk, approximately
peppermint essence
100g dark chocolate, melted, extra
30g unsalted butter, melted, extra

Into 20cm square cake pan place strip of foil to line base and extend over 2 opposite ends. Combine chocolate and butter in small bowl, stir until smooth. Spread evenly over base of prepared pan; refrigerate until set.

Combine sifted icing sugar and oil in heatproof bowl, stir in enough milk to make a stiff paste; flavour with essence. Stir constantly over hot water until spreadable. Spread evenly over chocolate base; refrigerate until set.

Combine extra chocolate and extra butter in small bowl, stir until smooth; cool until spreadable. Spread chocolate mixture over peppermint filling; refrigerate until set. Lift mixture from pan, gently peel away foil, place chocolate on board, cut into shapes.

WHITE CHOCOLATE PETIT FOURS

Grand Marnier is an orange-flavoured liqueur. Petit fours can be prepared up to a day ahead; keep, covered, in refrigerator. Serve at room temperature. Recipe unsuitable to freeze or microwave.

SPONGE
3 eggs
½ cup castor sugar
¼ cup cornflour
¼ cup plain flour
¼ cup self-raising flour
30g dark chocolate, melted
GRAND MARNIER SYRUP
½ cup water
¼ cup sugar
2 tablespoons Grand Marnier
WHITE CHOCOLATE FILLING
2 egg whites
¼ cup castor sugar
200g unsalted butter
1 teaspoon grated orange rind
150g White Melts, melted

Sponge: Grease 25cm x 30cm Swiss roll pan, line base and sides with paper, grease paper. Beat eggs in small bowl with electric mixer until thick and creamy (about 7 minutes). Gradually add sugar a little at a time, beat after each addition until sugar is dissolved. Sift dry ingredients together 3 times.

Transfer egg mixture to large bowl, sift flours over egg mixture, lightly fold flours through egg mixture.

Spread mixture evenly into prepared pan, bake in moderate oven for about 15 minutes or until just firm. Turn immediately onto wire rack to cool, turn sponge right way up.

Cut sponge in half vertically. Place half on serving plate, brush with half the syrup, spread with half the filling. Top with remaining sponge, syrup and filling. Cut cake into desired shapes, drizzle or pipe with dark chocolate.

Grand Marnier Syrup: Combine water and sugar in small saucepan, stir over heat, without boiling, until sugar is dissolved; bring to boil, reduce heat, simmer, uncovered, without stirring, for 3 minutes; add liqueur, cool to room temperature.

White Chocolate Filling: Beat egg whites in small bowl until soft peaks form. Gradually add sugar, beat until dissolved. Beat butter and rind in small bowl with electric mixer until as white as possible, beat in egg white mixture in 2 batches. Beat in White Melts.

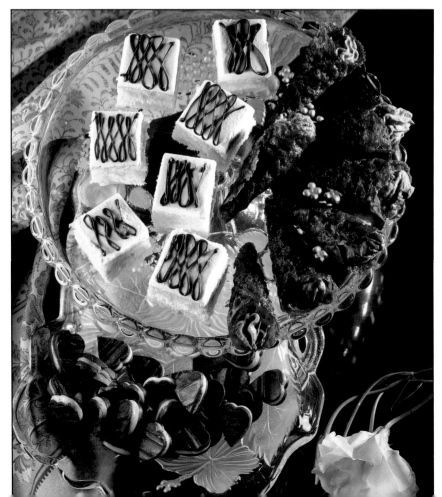

LEFT: Above, from left: White Chocolate Petit Fours; Honey Snap Cones with Chocolate Cream; below: Chocolate Thins. ABOVE, RIGHT: White and Dark Chocolate Roll.

Glassware: Mikasa; fabric: Les Olivades (left)

WHITE AND DARK CHOCOLATE ROLL

Roll can be made a week ahead; keep, covered, in refrigerator. Recipe unsuitable to freeze or microwave.

250g butter
1 teaspoon vanilla essence
¾ cup castor sugar
7 eggs, separated
⅔ cup plain flour
2 tablespoons cornflour
200g dark chocolate, melted
¼ cup castor sugar, extra
WHITE CHOCOLATE FILLING
300g white chocolate, melted
30g butter, melted
CHOCOLATE ICING
90g dark chocolate, melted
15g butter, melted

Grease 25cm x 30cm Swiss roll pan, cover base with paper, grease paper. Combine butter, essence and sugar in medium bowl, beat with electric mixer until light and fluffy, add egg yolks, beat until combined. Beat in sifted flours on low speed. Divide batter into 2 large bowls; stir the cooled chocolate into 1 of the bowls.

Beat egg whites in medium bowl with electric mixer until soft peaks form; gradually add extra sugar, beat until dissolved. Divide egg white mixture equally between the bowls of plain and chocolate batters, fold in gently in 2 batches.

Spread ½ cup of the chocolate batter into the prepared pan (layer will be very thin). Grill for 45 seconds to 2 minutes or until chocolate batter is baked through and lightly browned. Spread ½ cup of the plain batter on top of the baked chocolate layer and grill as before.

Repeat this 4 times, building up 10 layers. Immediately turn cake onto teatowel, remove lining paper, roll cake firmly in greaseproof paper, cool.

When cold, unroll and spread with filling, then re-roll. Wrap roll in foil, refrigerate for 1 hour. Remove roll from refrigerator, spread all over with chocolate icing, refrigerate until set.
White Chocolate Filling: Combine chocolate and butter in small bowl, stir until smooth and spreadable.
Chocolate Icing: Combine chocolate and butter in small bowl, stir until smooth and spreadable.

Cover base of 19cm x 29cm lamington pan with paper, grease paper. Combine Milk Melts, golden syrup, butter and cream in large saucepan, stir constantly over heat, without boiling, until chocolate is melted. Stir in biscuits, almonds and coconut. Press mixture into prepared pan, spread with topping, refrigerate 1 hour or until set before cutting.

Topping: Combine chocolate and butter in small bowl, stir until smooth and spreadable.

COFFEE THINS

Thins can be flavoured with orange rind and Grand Marnier, if preferred. Tia Maria and Kahlua are coffee-flavoured liqueurs. Thins can be prepared up to a week ahead; keep, covered, in refrigerator. This recipe is unsuitable to freeze.

250g dark chocolate, melted
60g unsalted butter, melted
1 teaspoon dry instant coffee
2 tablespoons Tia Maria or Kahlua

Grease deep 19cm square cake pan, line with foil, grease foil. Combine chocolate, butter and combined coffee and liqueur in small bowl, stir until smooth. Pour into prepared pan; cover, refrigerate until set, remove from pan, cut into desired shapes. Refrigerate before serving.

Orange Thins: Substitute 1 teaspoon grated orange rind for the 1 teaspoon dry instant coffee, and Grand Marnier for Tia Maria.

CHOCOLATE NUT SLICE

Slice can be kept in an airtight container in refrigerator for up to a week. Recipe unsuitable to freeze.

50g white chocolate, finely chopped
300g dark chocolate, melted
¾ cup sweetened condensed milk
½ cup toasted almonds
½ cup pistachio nuts
½ cup pecans or walnuts
1 tablespoon brandy

Line 8cm x 26cm bar pan with foil. Sprinkle white chocolate into prepared pan. Combine dark chocolate, milk, nuts and brandy in bowl, mix well; spread evenly over white chocolate. Cover, refrigerate several hours or overnight. Slice thinly, refrigerate before serving.

CHOCOLATE MALLOWS

Slice can be prepared up to 2 days ahead; keep, covered, in refrigerator. This recipe is not suitable to freeze or microwave.

½ cup brown sugar
½ cup plain flour
¾ cup sweetened condensed milk
100g milk chocolate, chopped
60g butter
50g white marshmallows
2 tablespoons cream
½ cup pecans or walnuts, chopped
1 cup shortbread biscuit crumbs
CHOCOLATE GLAZE
125g dark chocolate, melted
60g unsalted butter, melted

Into 19cm x 29cm lamington pan place strip of foil to cover base and extend over 2 opposite ends. Blend sugar and flour with milk in saucepan, add chocolate, butter, marshmallows and cream; stir constantly over heat, without boiling, until chocolate is melted and sugar is dissolved.

Bring to boil, remove from heat, stir in nuts and biscuit crumbs. Pour into prepared pan, refrigerate until set. Spread with glaze, refrigerate until set before cutting.

Chocolate Glaze: Combine chocolate and butter in small bowl, stir until smooth and spreadable.

CARAMEL BISCUIT BITES

Sweets can be made a week ahead, keep, covered, in refrigerator. Recipe unsuitable to freeze.

200g Milk Melts
2 tablespoons golden syrup
185g butter
2 tablespoons cream
250g packet plain sweet biscuits, chopped
2 cups (200g) flaked almonds, chopped
⅔ cup flaked coconut, chopped
TOPPING
150g milk chocolate, melted
15g butter, melted

ABOVE, LEFT: Caramel Biscuit Bites.
RIGHT: Clockwise from top left:
Chocolate Nut Slice; Chocolate Mallows;
Coffee Thins; Orange Thins.

CHOCOLATE STOLLEN

Marzipan can be bought in 200g rolls from delicatessens, health food stores and some supermarkets. Stollen can be prepared up to 2 days ahead or frozen for up to 2 months. Recipe unsuitable to microwave.

⅓ cup sultanas
1 tablespoon dark rum
30g compressed yeast
¼ cup castor sugar
⅓ cup milk, warmed
2 cups plain flour
1 teaspoon mixed spice
1 egg, lightly beaten
60g butter, melted
1 teaspoon vanilla essence
⅓ cup blanched almonds
60g dark chocolate, chopped
60g milk chocolate, chopped
½ teaspoon grated lemon rind
100g marzipan
30g butter, melted, extra
1 tablespoon icing sugar

Combine sultanas and rum in bowl, stand several hours or overnight.

Combine yeast, 1 tablespoon of the sugar and milk in small bowl, cover; stand in warm place until foamy.

Sift flour and spice into large bowl, make well in centre, stir in remaining sugar, yeast mixture, egg, butter, essence, rum and sultanas, beat well with wooden spoon. Turn onto lightly floured surface, knead well for about 5 minutes. Place dough into lightly oiled bowl, cover, stand in warm place for about 40 minutes or until dough has doubled in size.

Turn dough onto lightly floured surface, knead in nuts, both chocolates and rind. Shape dough into a 25cm round. Make marzipan into a sausage-shaped roll the same length as the dough. Place roll just off centre on dough, fold dough almost in half, flatten slightly with hand. Place onto lightly greased oven tray, stand, covered, in warm place for about 20 minutes or until increased in size by half. Brush stollen with half the extra butter.

Bake in moderate oven for about 45 minutes or until stollen sounds hollow when tapped. Brush with remaining butter and dust with sifted icing sugar before serving warm or cold.

CHOCOLATE DOUGHNUTS

Doughnuts are best served the day they are made; they can be frozen, without sugar coating, for 2 months. Recipe unsuitable to microwave.

15g compressed yeast
⅔ cup warm milk
⅓ cup castor sugar
2½ cups plain flour
2 tablespoons cocoa
1 teaspoon ground cinnamon
30g butter, melted
2 eggs, lightly beaten
½ cup Choc Bits
oil for deep frying
extra castor sugar

Blend yeast with a little of the warm milk, stir in remaining milk and 1 tablespoon of the sugar; stand in warm place for about 10 minutes or until foamy. Sift flour, cocoa, cinnamon and remaining sugar into large bowl. Make well in centre, stir in butter, eggs, Choc Bits and yeast mixture; mix to a soft dough. Turn dough into clean, lightly-oiled bowl; cover, stand in warm place for about 40 minutes or until the mixture has doubled in size.

Turn dough onto lightly floured surface, knead for about 5 minutes or until smooth and elastic. Roll dough on floured surface to about 1cm thickness. Cut out with 8cm cutter, cut out centres with 2½cm cutter.

Place doughnuts and centres on lightly greased oven trays, cover, stand in warm place for about 20 minutes or until increased in size by half. Heat oil, deep-fry doughnuts a few at a time until golden brown and cooked through; turn frequently. Drain doughnuts on absorbent paper; toss in extra castor sugar.

Makes about 10.

ABOVE: Chocolate Stollen.

Glass: Mikasa

CHOCOLATE HAZELNUT PINWHEELS

Pinwheels are best eaten on the day they are made. Uniced pinwheels can be frozen for up to 2 months. Recipe unsuitable to microwave.

30g compressed yeast
¼ cup warm water
1 teaspoon castor sugar
60g butter
¼ cup castor sugar, extra
1 egg yolk
2 cups plain flour
½ teaspoon ground cinnamon
¼ cup cream, warmed
60g butter, extra
⅓ cup brown sugar
1 cup roasted hazelnuts, chopped
¾ cup Choc Bits
¼ cup roasted hazelnuts, chopped, extra
COFFEE ICING
¾ cup icing sugar
15g butter
2 teaspoons dry instant coffee
2 tablespoons boiling water

Lightly grease deep 20cm cake pan. Blend yeast and water together in small bowl, stir in sugar. Stand in warm place for about 10 minutes or until mixture is foamy.

Cream butter and extra sugar in small bowl with electric mixer until light and fluffy, add egg yolk, beat until

combined. Transfer to large bowl. Stir in sifted flour and cinnamon, cream and yeast mixture, mix to a soft dough. Turn dough onto lightly floured surface, knead for about 10 minutes or until dough is smooth and elastic. Place dough into bowl, cover, stand in warm place for about 40 minutes or until dough is doubled in size. Turn dough onto lightly floured surface, knead until smooth.

Roll the dough into rectangle measuring 26cm x 40cm.

Cream extra butter and brown sugar in bowl until combined, spread evenly over dough, sprinkle with hazelnuts and Choc Bits.

Roll up dough like a Swiss roll from the long side. Cut into 12 pieces, place into prepared pan. Cover, stand in warm place for about 20 minutes or until pinwheels are well risen. Bake in moderately hot oven for 10 minutes, reduce heat to moderate, bake further 25 minutes. Turn onto wire rack to cool. When cold, drizzle with icing, sprinkle with extra hazelnuts.

Coffee Icing: Sift icing sugar into small bowl, stir in butter and combined coffee and water, mix well.

LEFT: Chocolate Doughnuts.
ABOVE: Chocolate Hazelnut Pinwheels.

Plate: Lifestyle Imports; table: Country Style Interiors (left). China: Villeroy & Boch; table & fabric: Australian East India Co. (above)

Glossary

*Some terms, names and alternatives
are included here to help everyone use
our recipes perfectly.*

AFTER-DINNER MINTS: we used square thin chocolates filled with a mint-flavoured fondant cream.

ARROWROOT: a thickening ingredient; cornflour can be substituted.

BAKING PAPER: can be used to line cake pans, making piping bags, etc. It is not necessary to grease after lining pans.

BICARBONATE OF SODA: baking soda, a component of baking powder.

BREADCRUMBS: stale: use 1 or 2 day old white bread made into crumbs by grating, blending or processing. **Packaged:** use commercially packaged breadcrumbs.

BUTTER: we used salted butter (sweet) unless otherwise specified; good quality cooking margarine can be used; 125g butter is equal to 1 stick butter.

BUTTERMILK: the liquid left from the milk from which cream was made. It is now made by adding culture to skim milk to give a slightly acid flavour; skim milk can be substituted, if preferred.

CARAMEL TOPPING: a flavouring used in milk drinks or on ice-cream.

CHESTNUT PUREE: an unsweetened purée of chestnuts. Do not confuse with the sweetened flavoured chestnut spread.

CHOC BITS (morsels): are small buds of dark chocolate available in 100g and 250g packets; these do not melt when cooked in food such as biscuits and cakes, etc. One metric measuring cup will hold about 155g.

CHOC MELTS (compounded chocolate): are discs of dark compounded chocolate available in 375g packets; these are ideal for melting and moulding. One metric measuring cup will hold about 155g.

COCOA: cocoa powder.

COCONUT: use desiccated unless otherwise specified.

COCONUT CREAM: available in cans and cartons in supermarkets and Asian stores; coconut milk can be substituted although it is not as thick.

COLOURINGS: we used concentrated liquid vegetable food colourings in our recipes.

COMPRESSED YEAST: 3 level teaspoons dried yeast can be substituted for 30g compressed yeast.

CORNFLOUR: cornstarch.

CORN SYRUP: an imported product available in supermarkets, delicatessens and health food stores. It is available in light or dark — either can be substituted for the other.

CREAM: we have specified thickened (whipping) cream when necessary in recipes; cream is simply a light pouring cream, also known as half 'n' half.
Sour: a thick commercially cultured soured cream.
Light sour: a less dense commercially cultured soured cream; do not substitute this for sour cream.

CUSTARD POWDER: pudding mix.

DARK CHOCOLATE: we used dark club (dark eating) chocolate available in 50g, 200g and 250g blocks.

DARK RUM: we prefer to use an underproof rum (not overproof) for a more subtle flavour.

ESSENCE: extract.

FLOUR: plain flour: all-purpose flour. **Self-raising flour:** substitute plain (all-purpose) flour and baking powder in the proportion of ¾ metric cup plain flour to 2 level metric teaspoons baking powder; sift together several times. If using an 8oz measuring cup, use 1 cup plain flour to 2 level metric teaspoons baking powder.

FRUIT MINCE: mincemeat.

GLACE GINGER: crystallised ginger can be substituted; rinse off the sugar with warm water, dry well before using.

GLUCOSE SYRUP (liquid glucose): is made from wheat starch; it is available at health food stores and some supermarkets.

GOLDEN SYRUP: maple/pancake syrup or honey can be substituted.

GREASEPROOF PAPER: we used this paper to line cake pans, etc; do not confuse with the shiny wax paper. It is best to grease greaseproof paper after lining the pan. Also see Baking Paper for lining pans.

GRILL, GRILLER: broil, broiler.

GROUND ALMONDS/ HAZELNUTS: we used packaged commercially ground nuts in our recipes unless otherwise specified.

JAM: conserve.

LAMINGTON PAN: a rectangular slab pan with a depth of 4cm.

LIQUEURS: we have used a variety of liqueurs; if desired, you can use brandy instead (however, the flavour will change). If alcohol is not desirable, substitute with fruit juice of an equivalent flavour or milk or water to balance the liquid proportions in the recipe.

MACAROON: a crisp biscuit made from coconut, egg white and sugar. They can also be bought almond-flavoured.

MARSALA: a sweet fortified wine.

MILK BITS (morsels): are small buds of milk chocolate available in 100g and 250g packets; these do not melt when cooked in food such as biscuits and cakes, etc. One metric measuring cup will hold about 155g.

MILK CHOCOLATE: available in 50g, 200g and 250g blocks.

MILK MELTS: are discs of milk compounded chocolate available in 375g packets; these are ideal for melting and moulding. One metric cup will hold 155g.

MIXED PEEL: a mixture of chopped crystallised citrus peel.

MIXED SPICE: a finely ground combination of spices which includes allspice, nutmeg and cinnamon; used as an ingredient in sweet recipes.

OIL: we used a light polyunsaturated salad oil unless otherwise stated.

PUNNET: small basket usually holding about 250g fruit.

RED CURRANT JELLY: a sweet preserve made from red currants.

RICE BUBBLES: rice crispies.

SAVOIARDI BISCUITS: also known as Savoy biscuits, lady's fingers or sponge fingers, they are Italian-style crisp fingers made from sponge cake mixture.

SUGAR: we used coarse granulated table sugar also known as crystal sugar unless otherwise specified.
Castor: fine granulated table sugar.
Icing: confectioners' or powdered sugar. We used icing sugar mixture (not pure) in the recipes in this book.

SULTANAS: seedless white raisins.

SWEET BISCUITS: any plain sweet biscuit (or cookie) can be used; chocolate biscuits used were uniced.

SWEETENED CONDENSED MILK: we used Nestlé's milk which has had 60 percent of the water removed, then sweetened with sugar.

WEET-BIX: Weetabix or Ruskets.

WHITE CHOCOLATE: we used Milky Bar, which is available in 50g, 200g and 250g blocks.

WHITE MELTS: are discs of white compounded chocolate available in 375g packets; these are ideal for melting or moulding. One metric measuring cup will hold about 155g.

WHITE RUM: we used Bacardi rum, which is colourless.

Tips for Success

Here are the simplest ways to handle chocolate as used in our recipes, plus how to create tempting decorative effects.

TO MICROWAVE CHOCOLATE:

Break up blocks of chocolate or spread melts in a single layer onto a plate. Microwave on HIGH until the chocolate is soft. Remember, it will still hold most of its shape even when it is melted, as shown above. The time it takes to melt will depend on the oven and the amount to be melted.; start checking after 30 seconds.

CHOCOLATE CURLS:

Melt chocolate, either dark or Melts, spread in a thin layer over a cool surface, such as ceramic tile, granite or marble, allow to set at room temperature. Holding a large sharp knife at about a 45° angle, pull it gently over the surface of the chocolate to form curls.

SHAVED CHOCOLATE:

Use a vegetable peeler to make quick mini curls of chocolate from the block.

CHOCOLATE SHAPES:

Spread a thin layer of chocolate or Melts onto baking paper or foil, allow to set at room temperature; use sharp cutter or a knife to cut out shapes.

CHOCOLATE

TO MELT CHOCOLATE

We have used Nestlés chocolate throughout this book; some varieties are designed to melt, but others retain their chunky shape. Here we give tips on how to melt chocolate successfully:

THERE ARE 2 KEY POINTS:

1. As general rule, do not allow water to come in contact with chocolate when it is heating. Just a drop of water is the danger; a larger amount of liquid usually blends in smoothly, as you will see we specify in certain recipes.

2. Do not over-heat chocolate.

If either happens and the chocolate turns from a glossy, liquid mass to a dull, coarse, textured mess, you will have to discard the chocolate and start again.

If chocolate is melted correctly, and you have some left over, it can be remelted over and over again.

Chocolate should never be melted by itself over direct heat. Instead, choose a double saucepan or heatproof bowl over a saucepan of water. Place chocolate in the top of the saucepan or the bowl and then set it aside.

Put water into the bottom half of the saucepan, but not enough to touch the base of the top saucepan or bowl. Bring water to boil, remove from heat then immediately place the chocolate in its saucepan or bowl over the hot water. Leave to stand, stirring occasionally, until the chocolate is smooth.

Do not cover the bowl containing the chocolate or condensation will form, then water will drop into the chocolate and it will be ruined.

SETTING CHOCOLATE:

Chocolate sets best at a fairly cool temperatures of around 17°C (65°F); however, it will set at average room temperature of about 21°C (72°F). This takes longer but chocolate will hold its shape and gloss well. If the room temperature is too warm, then refrigeration of the chocolate is the only answer. This will cause chocolate to "sweat: and lose its gloss. Melts are the easiest and quickest to set.

CHOCOLATE LEAVES:

Many leaves are suitable; wash and dry them before using. Brush surface with a melted chocolate of Melts, allow to set at room temperature, if possible. Peel leaves from chocolate. Melts will retain their shape at room temperature. Dark, milk or white chocolate leaves will have to be refrigerated to retain their shape.

CHOCOLATE-DIPPED STRAWBERRIES OR NUTS:

Melt about 100g chocolate or Melts and dip berries into the warm chocolate. Stand on foil-covered tray, refrigerate until set.

CHOCOLATE PALM TREES:

Using melted chocolate or Melts, pipe leaves, onto baking paper or foil, then trunks as shown. Leave to set at room temperature for best results.

CHOCOLATE LACE:

Draw shapes onto baking paper or foil, use chocolate or Melts to pipe outline of lace wedges, then fill in with lacy lines, allow to set at room temperature for best results.

TOFFEE AND PRALINE

Toffee is made from browned sugar; praline (which always contains nuts) is made by crushing the toffee after it is set. Some recipes start with only sugar; others have water added but this is evaporated during the boiling process.

TOFFEE:

We used a heavy-based frying pan for best results. Add the sugar, place over high heat and move the pan around so the sugar melts and browns evenly. It is safest not to stir at this stage.

Picture above shows sugar almost dissolved and turning brown.

If using water and sugar, stir the mixture constantly over high heat, without boiling, until every sugar grain is dissolved. If any grains cling to the side of the pan or wooden spoon, brush them into the syrup with a wet pastry brush.

Let the syrup come to the boil, boil rapidly, still over high heat, without stirring, until the syrup turns a light golden brown or to the colour indicated in individual recipes. Stirring at this stage could crystallise the mixture and you will have to throw it out and start again.

PRALINE:

Drop nuts into the toffee when the toffee is as brown as desired, do not stir; pour immediately onto lightly oiled tray. Leave to set at room temperature; do not refrigerate. Chop, blend or process until the praline is as fine as required. Leftover praline will keep for months in a sealed jar at room temperature.

TOFFEE-DIPPED NUTS:

Hold nuts with two skewers or two forks, dip nuts into toffee, place onto foil-covered tray to set.

TOFFEE SHAPES:

Spoonfuls of toffee make wonderful abstract designs. Spoon toffee onto lightly oiled oven tray, leave to set before removing from tray. Do not refrigerate or toffee will break down and liquefy.

TOFFEE LACE

Drizzle spoonfuls of toffee into threads on a lightly oiled oven tray. This sets almost immediately, and can be snapped into pretty pieces. Do not refrigerate or toffee will break down and liquefy.

PIPING

Piping is a simple way to decorate cakes, biscuits, etc, with icing, melted chocolate and whipped cream; generally a piping bag fitted with tube or a paper piping bag is used.

HOW TO MAKE A PAPER PIPING BAG:

Use greaseproof paper or baking paper. Cut paper into triangles, twist into a cone shape, fold over the top, as shown, or secure with clear adhesive tape. Place icing, chocolate or cream in bag, snip a tiny hole in the tip of the bag. Gently ease icing down into bag, fold over top, enlarge hole with scissors to required size.

HOW TO FILL PIPING BAG FITTED WITH TUBE:

We use large pastry bags made from a synthetic fabric or calico. There are many sizes and types available, all are adequate. There are also many sizes and patterns of tubes available in metal or plastic. Metal tends to be better for fluted pipes, as the design is sharper; however, they are more expensive than the plastic.

Place cream or butter into bag.

STARS:

Hold bag between thumb and first finger, twist top, then hold firmly in hand. For stars, hold bag upright and squeeze bag to make stars of desired size.

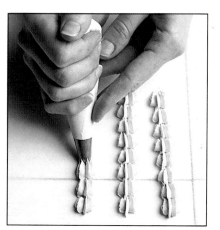

SHELLS:

Hold bag at about 45° angle and use backwards and forwards movements for shell shapes. It takes only a little practice.

DECORATION

FEATHER AND FAN EFFECT:

This effective decoration is made by piping lines of icing or chocolate evenly onto the surface of icing or cream. It is important that both the surface and the piped icing are soft while making the pattern. Pull a skewer through the lines of icing in one direction, then the opposite direction, as shown.

CHOCOLATE TUILES:

Pipe lines of plain mixture over chocolate mixture; use a skewer, as shown, to make the feather and fan pattern.

CITRUS PEEL STRANDS:

These can be done several hours ahead of using. Use finely shredded rind from any citrus fruit; avoid using any white pith. Place ½ cup sugar in frying pan or saucepan, add ¼ cup water, stir constantly over heat, without boiling, until sugar is dissolved. Bring to boil, boil rapidly, uncovered, until sugar syrup turns light golden brown. Add rind, simmer for about 5 minutes. Remove rind from syrup to tray to cool before using.

TO TOAST COCONUT:

There are several methods of toasting coconut; we find this the most efficient. Place about 1 cup coconut in small heavy-based frying pan. Stir constantly over medium heat until coconut is light golden brown, turn immediately onto heatproof tray to cool before using. Leftover toasted coconut will keep indefinitely in an airtight container in the refrigerator.

Index

G

Ginger Bites, Pineapple	115
Ginger Florentines, Apricot	22
Ginger Tartlets, Macadamia	88
Glacé Fruit Nuggets	3
Glazed Chocolate Apricot Roll	45
Golden Coconut Slice	14

H

Hazelnut Apricot Truffles	108
Hazelnut Clusters	113
Hazelnut Coffee Log	56
Hazelnut Pinwheels, Chocolate	121
Hazelnut Steamed Pudding, Chocolate	93
Hazelnut Torte, Caramel	49
Hazelnut Torte, Double Chocolate	47
Heaps of Chocolate	22
Heavenly Raspberry Marshmallow Slice	18
Honey Cream Chocolate Sponge	34
Honey Mousse, White Chocolate and	73
Honey Snap Cones with Chocolate Cream	116
Honey Sponge, Chocolate	58
Hot Chocolate Soufflés with Cherry Cream	84

I

Ice-Cream Bombe, Coffee Truffle	82
Ice-Cream, Chocolate Pecan Dream	92
Ice-Cream Ring, Chocolate Mandarin	76

J

Jewel Delights	115

L

Lamington Butterfly Sponge	54
Lemon and Nut Chocolate Cake	50
Lemon Cheesecake with Chocolate Glaze	64
Liqueur Cake, Chocolate Almond	35
Liqueur Cups, Cherry	109
Liqueur Dream Cake, Peachy	32

M

Macadamia Ginger Tartlets	88
Macadamia Praline Slice	12
Macaroon Puddings, Walnut	81
Macaroons, Peppermint	4
Mallow Rounds, Pecan	115
Mallows, Chocolate	118
Mallow Slice, Minty	15
Mandarin Ice-Cream Ring, Chocolate	76
Marsala Cake, Chocolate	56
Marshmallow Crowns, Chocolate	8
Marshmallow Slice, Cherry	108
Marshmallow Slice, Heavenly Raspberry	18
Marzipan Chocolates	110
Marzipan Slice, Coconut	20
Meringue Cake, Almond	39
Meringue Dacquoise, Chocolate Strawberry	92
Meringue Desserts, Chocolate Cherry	76
Meringue Flans, Chocolate and Berry	87
Meringue Torte with Custard Cream, Almond	74
Milk Chocolate Rum 'n' Raisin Mousse	96
Minted Chocolate Flan	70
Minted Flan, Chocolate	70
Mint Squares, Chocolate	19

Mint Surprises, Almond	96
Minty Mallow Slice	15
Mocha Bavarian with Pecan Praline	73
Mocha Chequerboard Mousse	100
Mocha Gateau, Rich	51
Mocha Mousse, Frozen	99
Mocha Torte with Chocolate Lace, Almond	49
Mocha Truffle Cake	25
Moist Chocolate Carrot Cake	29
Moist Coffee Cake with Chocolate Syrup	36
Mousse, Brandy Snap Baskets with Currant Liqueur	90
Mousse, Frozen Mocha	99
Mousse, Milk Chocolate Rum 'n' Raisin	96
Mousse, Mocha Chequerboard	100
Mousse Sponge, Chocolate	42
Mousse, White Chocolate and Honey	73
Mousse with Strawberry Sauce, Frozen Chocolate	80

N

Nougat, Chocolate	103
Nut Bread, Chocolate Fruit and	105
Nut Cake, The Unbelievably Rich Chocolate	52
Nut Chocolate Cake, Lemon and	50
Nut Cluster Bars	19
Nut Fudge, Chocolate Marshmallow	106
Nuts, Chocolate	113
Nut Slice, Chocolate	118
Nutty Chocolate Clusters	106
Nutty Surprises, Chocolate	4

O

Orange Cheesecake, Chocolate	83
Orange Sour Cream Cake, Choc-Chip	45
Orange Thins	118

P

Palmiers, Chocolate	110
Passionfruit Cream of Hearts	88
Passionfruit Satin Cake	60
Peachy Liqueur Dream Cake	32
Peanut Butter Cake, Chocolate	34
Peanut Soft Centres	104
Peanut Squares	112
Peanutties, Chocolate	16
Pear Puff, Chocolate	99
Pears with Cointreau and Passionfruit Syrup	91
Pecan Crêpes with Coffee Sauce	86
Pecan Dream Ice-Cream, Chocolate	92
Pecan Flan, Chunky Chocolate	72
Pecan Mallow Rounds	115
Pecan Pie, Chocolate	74
Pecan Tartlets, Chocolate Cream	110
Peppermint Chocolate Ring	29
Peppermint Macaroons	4
Petit Fours, White Chocolate	116
Pineapple Chocolate Squares	14
Pineapple Ginger Bites	115
Pistachio Biscuits, Chocolate	10
Pistachio Truffles, Coconut	104
Poppy Seed Cake, Chocolate	38
Praline Slice, Macadamia	12
Pretzels, Chocolate	7
Pudding, Chocolate Hazelnut Steamed	93
Puddings, Walnut Macaroon	81
Puffs, Chocolate Toffee	70

R

Raisin Caramel Bars, Rum	16
Raisin Mousse, Milk Chocolate Rum 'n'	96

Raspberry Lace Baskets	84
Raspberry Marshmallow Slice, Heavenly	18
Raspberry Towers, Chocolate	78
Rice Ring, Tropical	100
Rich Dark Chocolate Mint Fudge	106
Rich Mocha Gateau	51
Rocky Road Biscuits	8
Roughs, Chocolate Marble	106
Rum Chocolate Creams	6
Rum Dessert, Almond	94
Rum 'n' Raisin Mousse, Milk Chocolate	96
Rum Raisin Caramel Bars	16
Rum Truffles, Chocolate	109

S

Sauce, Chocolate Fudge	64
Saucy Chocolate Almond Desserts	68
Shortbread, Chocolate	16
Soufflés, Frozen Chocolate and Coconut	67
Soufflés with Cherry Cream, Hot Chocolate	84
Sour Cream Cake, Apricot	25
Sour Cream Cake, Choc-Chip Orange	45
Spice Cake, Sugar 'n'	58
Sponge, Brandied Walnut	62
Sponge, Chocolate Mousse	42
Sponge, Honey Chocolate	58
Sponge, Honey Cream Chocolate	34
Sponge, Lamington Butterfly	54
Stollen, Chocolate	120
Strawberry Meringue Dacquoise, Chocolate	92
Sugar 'n' Spice Cake	58

T

Tartlets, Chocolate Cream Pecan	110
Tartlets, Macadamia Ginger	88
The Unbelievably Rich Chocolate Nut Cake	52
Thins, Chocolate	116
Thins, Coffee	118
Thins, Orange	118
Toffee Almond Cherries	103
Toffee Puffs, Chocolate	70
Torte Royale	30
Tropical Rice Ring	100
Truffle Cake, Mocha	25
Truffle Ice-Cream Bombe, Coffee	82
Truffles, Chocolate Rum	109
Truffles, Coconut Pistachio	104
Truffles, Hazelnut Apricot	108
Tuile Rolls with White Chocolate Filling	4
Tuiles, Chocolate	3
Two-Tone Biscuits	7

W

Walnut Log, Chocolate	41
Walnut Macaroon Puddings	81
Walnut Sponge, Brandied	62
White and Dark Chocolate Roll	117
White Chocolate and Honey Mousse	73
White Chocolate Bars, Fruity	10
White Chocolate Petit Fours	116
White Chocolate Ripple Cake	30

Y

Yoghurt Cake with Red Currant Cream, Chocolate	52

Z

Zabaglione, Chocolate	68

QUICK CONVERSION GUIDE

Wherever you live in the world, you can use our recipes with the help of our easy-to-follow conversions for all your cooking needs. These conversions are approximate only. The difference between the exact and approximate conversions of liquid and dry measures amounts to only a teaspoon or two, and will not make any noticeable difference to your cooking results.

MEASURING EQUIPMENT

The difference between measuring cups internationally is minimal within 2 or 3 teaspoons' difference. (For the record, 1 Australian metric measuring cup will hold approximately 250ml.) The most accurate way of measuring dry ingredients is to weigh them. When measuring liquids use a clear glass or plastic jug with metric markings.

In this book we use metric measuring cups and spoons approved by Standards Australia.
- a graduated set of 4 cups for measuring dry ingredients; the sizes are marked on the cups.
- a graduated set of 4 spoons for measuring dry and liquid ingredients; the amounts are marked on the spoons.
- 1 TEASPOON: 5ml
- 1 TABLESPOON: 20ml

NOTE: NZ, CANADA, USA AND UK ALL USE 15ml TABLESPOONS.
ALL CUP AND SPOON MEASUREMENTS ARE LEVEL.

DRY MEASURES

METRIC	IMPERIAL
15g	½oz
30g	1oz
60g	2oz
90g	3oz
125g	4oz (¼lb)
155g	5oz
185g	6oz
220g	7oz
250g	8oz (½lb)
280g	9oz
315g	10oz
345g	11oz
375g	12oz (¾lb)
410g	13oz
440g	14oz
470g	15oz
500g	16oz (1lb)
750g	24oz (1½lb)
1kg	32oz (2lb)

LIQUID MEASURES

METRIC	IMPERIAL
30ml	1 fluid oz
60ml	2 fluid oz
100ml	3 fluid oz
125ml	4 fluid oz
150ml	5 fluid oz (¼ pint/1 gill)
190ml	6 fluid oz
250ml	8 fluid oz
300ml	10 fluid oz (½ pint)
500ml	16 fluid oz
600ml	20 fluid oz (1 pint)
1000ml (1 litre)	1¾ pints

WE USE LARGE EGGS WITH AN AVERAGE WEIGHT OF 60g

HELPFUL MEASURES

METRIC	IMPERIAL
3mm	⅛in
6mm	¼in
1cm	½in
2cm	¾in
2.5cm	1in
5cm	2in
6cm	2½in
8cm	3in
10cm	4in
13cm	5in
15cm	6in
18cm	7in
20cm	8in
23cm	9in
25cm	10in
28cm	11in
30cm	12in (1ft)

HOW TO MEASURE

When using the graduated metric measuring cups, it is important to shake the dry ingredients loosely into the required cup. Do not tap the cup on the bench, or pack the ingredients into the cup unless otherwise directed. Level top of cup with knife. When using graduated metric measuring spoons, level top of spoon with knife. When measuring liquids in the jug, place jug on flat surface, check for accuracy at eye level.

OVEN TEMPERATURES

These oven temperatures are only a guide; we've given you the lower degree of heat. Always check the manufacturer's manual.

	C° (Celsius)	F° (Fahrenheit)	Gas Mark
Very slow	120	250	1
Slow	150	300	2
Moderately slow	160	325	3
Moderate	180	350	4
Moderately hot	190	375	5
Hot	200	400	6
Very hot	230	450	7